In the columns below, the number on the left designates the year of birth, and the number on the right designates the year the subject turns 21.

Year of Birth = 21 years old			
1985	2006	1991	2012
1986	2007	1992	2013
1987	2008	1993	2014
1988	2009	1994	2015
1989	2010	1995	2016
1990	2011	1996	2017

Search & Seizure

Always adhere to State statutes & local guidelines!

1 Incident to arrest you may make a warrantless search of:
  ✓ Arrested person at time & place of arrest
  ✓ Area(s) into which he might reach for weapon or destroy evidence
  ✓ Adjacent area(s) from which a hiding person could attack you

2 You may make a warrantless search of a vehicle if:
  ✓ Vehicle was in motion or mobile when seized, and
  ✓ You have probable cause to believe it contains ⎯⎯⎯⎯⎯⎯⎯⎯ or evidence of a crime

3

9689⊅900MW

4 You may make a warrantless search during a "hot pursuit" if:
- ✓ Suspect has committed a serious crime, and
- ✓ You have reason to believe he is armed & dangerous
- ✓ Purpose of the search is for the safety of the public and / or yourself

In limited circumstances, you make a warrantless entry into a building while in "hot pursuit" of a felony suspect whom you believe is not armed, but will destroy evidence if not apprehended immediately.

5 You may make a warrantless search without probable cause if:
- ✓ You have obtained consent from the person whose rights will be affected by it, or
- ✓ You have obtained consent from the person who has the right & authority to act for the person whose rights will be affected by it
- ✓ Consent must be positive - silence is not consent

6 You may make a warrantless search for evidence if:
- ✓ You have probable cause to believe the evidence is within the area(s) to be searched, and
- ✓ You have a reasonable belief it will be destroyed or moved before a warrant can be obtained

Social Security Numbers

The first three (3) numbers of the Social Security Number designate the state of issue.

001-003	New Hampshire	520	Wyoming
004-007	Maine	521-524	Colorado
008-009	Vermont	525	New Mexico

   ✓ SWAT Team
   ✓ Hostage Negotiation Team
   ✓ Aircraft

6 Determine
   ✓ Number of hostages, suspects, and descriptions
   ✓ Type, number, range, of weapons available
   ✓ Mental / criminal / terrorist
   ✓ Determine if drugs or alcohol used
   ✓ Communication — phone, bull horn, face-to-face

7 Prepare
   ✓ Put fire & EMS on standby
   ✓ Injured officer evacuation plan
   ✓ Gas plan
   ✓ Hostage rescue plan
   ✓ Consider psychiatrist, minister, friend, family

8 Media Relations (see page 39 and page 66)

Natural Disaster

ENSURE OFFICER SAFETY

1 Scene Evaluation
   ✓ Type of disaster
   ✓ Size
   ✓ Loss of life
   ✓ Injury
   ✓ Property destruction

NOTE: If this is a large-scale disaster, refer to the Major Incident Guidelines on page 30.

2 Evacuation / Aid to Injured
3 Establish Command Post
   ✓ Interagency communication
   ✓ Task assignment
   ✓ Length

✓ Nature
4 **Restrict Access to Danger Area**
   ✓ Protection of evacuation property
   ✓ Establish large storage facility
5 **Establish Manpower & Equipment Needs**
   ✓ Rescue and medical personnel
   ✓ U.S. & State forestry
   ✓ Coast Guard
   ✓ Dispatchers for assistance in communications
6 **Contact Witnesses**
   ✓ Establish missing persons list
   ✓ Enter in NCIC
7 **Document Manpower and Equipment Usage for Later Reimbursement**
8 **Media Relations (see page 39 and page 66)**

Officer Shooting Incidents

ENSURE OFFICER SAFETY — TO ENSURE MAXIMUM PROTECTION OF INDIVIDUAL RIGHTS OF PERSONS AND PROPERTY, ANY SHOOTING INCIDENT INVOLVING A POLICE OFFICER SHOULD BE TREATED LIKE A CRIMINAL INVESTIGATION.

1 **Secure Scene**
   ✓ Secure officer's weapon & ammunition intact
   ✓ Re-issue replacement weapon immediately
   ✓ Ensure officer's legal rights
2 **Ensure PERSONAL Contact With Officer's Immediate Family**
3 **Contact Department Counselor**
   ✓ Consider critical incident stress debriefing
   ✓ Discourage officer from media contact
4 **Remove Officer From Scene**
   ✓ On scene statement from officer should be brief
   ✓ Detailed statement taken later

1 Secure Scene
   ✓ Check victim(s) for signs of life — summon EMS
   ✓ Control access to scene
   ✓ Maintain scene access log
   ✓ Enter scene by route least likely to destroy
     evidence
   ✓ Search warrants
2 Dying Declaration
   ✓ Victim believes death impending
   ✓ Tape record or written documentation
3 Scene Preservation
   ✓ Establish and secure perimeter
   ✓ Prevent intrusion
   ✓ Establish and maintain contamination list
   ✓ Protect trace evidence from environmental
     conditions
   ✓ Take Polaroid photographs of all persons
     present
4 Identify All Persons and Vehicles Present
   ✓ Reason there and removal of unauthorized
     persons
   ✓ Isolate witnesses, suspects, and victims
5 Prevent Destruction of Fragile Evidence on
  Persons
   ✓ Exigent circumstances
   ✓ Consent searches

6 Preliminary Statements
- ✓ Witnesses
- ✓ Suspect(s) — Miranda Warning
- ✓ EMS personnel who transported victim / suspect
- ✓ Tape / video record

7 Broadcast Suspect Information

8 Notification
- ✓ Responsible authorities
- ✓ Victim's family

9 Media Relations (see page 39 and page 66)

Hostage/Sniper

ENSURE OFFICER SAFETY

1 Officer Safety Equipment
- ✓ Vests / AR-15 / gas masks / tear gas / portable radios / outside lighting / spotting scope

2 Determine Location of Suspect and Hostages
- ✓ Confine structure
- ✓ Contain suspect
- ✓ Determine access routes into structure
- ✓ Use maximum protection for patrols
- ✓ Evacuate adjacent buildings / rooms if necessary
- ✓ Obtain floor plan

3 Isolate Area
- ✓ Incoming vehicles
- ✓ Pedestrians
- ✓ Be aware of live media coverage suspect can view

4 Set Up Command Post
- ✓ Specify route to get to command post
- ✓ Hostage / suspect information available to officers
- ✓ Notify officers of responsibilities if shots are fired

✓ Keep officer informed of investigation status
6 Media Relations (see page 39 and page 66)

The following guidelines are critical to your mental, physical, and spiritual well-being, following a critical incident such as an officer-involved shooting, traffic accident, or other traumatic event.

1 **Avoid Excessive Use of Prescription Medications**
   ✓ Eat Healthy Foods
   ✓ Avoid alcohol, caffeine, smoking, high fat & high sugar foods
2 **Avoid Media Contact & Media Reports of Incident**
3 **Do Not Alienate Family & Friends**
4 **Get Physical Exercise to Release Stress-Induced Toxins**
5 **Set a Schedule & Follow Through**
6 **Remain Active**
7 **Be With People You Trust**
   ✓ Tell your story as many times as you feel safe
8 **Identify Emotional Responses**
   ✓ Be aware of your methods of dealing with stress
   ✓ Seek professional counseling

Press Releases

For information on press releases for Major Incidents, refer to page 39.

1 **Provide timely information to an accredited representative of the media in accordance with departmental guidelines.**
2 **Information appropriate to release:**
   ✓ Arrested person's:
     • name
     • age

- residence
- employment
- marital status
- and other similar biographical information
- ✓ Charge(s)
- ✓ Bail
- ✓ Investigating agency and length of investigation
- ✓ Biographical info on complaining party and victim (use discretion)
- ✓ Circumstances of arrest
- ✓ Time, place, resistance, pursuit
- ✓ Weapons used to effect arrest

3 Information inappropriate to release
- ✓ Contents of admissions or confessions
- ✓ Opinions about person's character
- ✓ Guilt or innocence
- ✓ Opinions about evidence
- ✓ Statements regarding anticipated testimony
- ✓ Weapons used in crime
- ✓ Descriptions of evidence and lab analysis

Report Writing

ENSURE OFFICER SAFETY

1 Principals
- ✓ Use the first person "I" when writing reports
- ✓ Use names rather than abbreviations
- ✓ Use the active voice of the verb
- ✓ Use factual rather than opinion statements
- ✓ Use the past tense verb as the main verb in sentences "handcuffed", "saw", "said", "took", "told"
- ✓ Use simple, professional language
- ✓ Sort ideas for the reader

with Threatening Message Such as "Anthrax":
- ✓ DO NOT shake or empty contents of package / envelope
- ✓ Place in a plastic bag or container to prevent leakage
- ✓ Leave the room and close the door. Keep others from entering
- ✓ Wash hands with soap and water to prevent spread

7 **Envelope / Package with Powder Spills Onto Surface:**
- ✓ DO NOT try to clean up the substance
- ✓ Cover the spilled contents with anything—DO NOT remove the cover.
- ✓ Wash hands with soap and water
- ✓ Blow nose
- ✓ Remove contaminated clothing and place in a sealed plastic bag
- ✓ Shower with soap and water. DO NOT use bleach or other disinfectant on skin

8 **Consider Room Contamination by Aerosolization:** (e.g. small device-triggered, warning that air handling system is contaminated or that a biological agent has been released in public space)
- ✓ Turn off local fans or ventilation units in the area
- ✓ Leave area immediately
- ✓ Close the door / section area off to keep others away

Terror

EXPLOSION & BOMBING INVESTIGATION

ENSURE OFFICER SAFETY

1 Conduct a Preliminary Evaluation of the Scene:
- ✓ Establish a command post / implement ICS
- ✓ Request additional resources:
  - Bomb technicians
  - Hazardous materials
- ✓ Identify witnesses, victims, preserve evidence

2 Preserve potentially transient physical evidence:
- ✓ Evidence present on victims
- ✓ Evidence that may be compromised by weather

3 Exercise Scene Safety:
- ✓ Request additional resources to mitigate hazards
- ✓ Use appropriate protective equipment
- ✓ Qualified personnel conduct safety sweep of area
- ✓ Clearly mark hazard areas
- ✓ Designate safety zones to receive victims

WARNING: Beware of additional devices! The scene may contain secondary explosive devices designed specifically to kill or maim public safety responders. Do not touch any suspicious items. If a suspected item is located, immediately evacuate the area and contact bomb disposal personnel.

4 Administer Lifesaving Efforts:
- ✓ Initiate rescues of severely injured / trapped victims
- ✓ Evacuate ambulatory victims
- ✓ Perform triage / treat life-threatening injuries
- ✓ Leave fatalities and their surroundings undisturbed
- ✓ Do not remove fatalities without authorization

5 Select and Set Up Command Post:
- ✓ Neutral ground, outside perimeter

911 Communications Center	
American Red Cross	
Chemtrec Emergency #	1-800-424-9300
Chemtrec Non-emergency #	1-800-262-8200
Children's Services	
CISD Team	
Crisis Center	
Domestic Violence Shelter	
EMS	
HazMat Team	
Homeless Shelter	
Medical Examiner / Coroner	
National Response Center	1-800-424-8802
Poison Control Center	
Public Health Department	
Sexual Abuse/Rape Victim Hotline	
Translation Services	
Trauma Center	

Phone

RADIO FREQUENCIES

Primary Police Dispatch
Police Tactical Channel #1
Police Tactical Channel #2
Police Tactical Channel #3
Police Tactical Channel #4
Police Car to Car
Police Helicopter
Primary Fire Dispatch
Fire Tactical Channel #1
Fire Tactical Channel #2
Fire Tactical Channel #3
HazMat Team
EMS Communications
Air Medical Helicopter
Hospital Communications System
Medical Examiner
Public Works Department

2 Response to Credible Anthrax Threats / WMD Devices:
- ✓ Isolate and secure immediate area around substance
- ✓ Contact: FBI, EOD, Fire, and HazMat
- ✓ If powder is not contained — cover if possible
- ✓ Consider shutting down HVAC system
- ✓ Have responsible party / building maintenance supervisor available to assist emergency responders
- ✓ Coordinate appropriate evacuation plan
- ✓ Evacuate building occupants or those in immediate area of material / device to one of the following areas:

3 **Category A:** Direct exposure to material and / or report strange taste or odor.

4 **Category B:** No direct exposure, but in same building / vicinity of material.
- ✓ If possible, note presence of any unusual packages, devices or people in area while evacuating
- ✓ Have evacuees remain in holding areas until interviewed, decontaminated (as needed) and authorized to leave

NOTE: EVACUATE 500 FEET TO COVER

5 **Minimum Protection when Determining Event Credibility:**
- ✓ Avoid contact with material or device
- ✓ Conduct recon of suspected material / device from a distance and through interview with recipient / victim
- ✓ N-95 or N-100 respiratory protection mask
- ✓ Powder-free, non-latex gloves (wash hands for three (3) minutes using soap and warm water)
- ✓ "Street Clothes" w/ long sleeves and Tyvek® suit

ENSURE RESPONDER SAFETY

1 Initial Screening:

✓ Is there a written threat with the package?
✓ Was there any other associated threat?
✓ Is it part of another device such as an improvised explosive device?
✓ Are there medical indications concerning a hazardous material exposure?
✓ Is there...

Excessive postage	Incorrect titles
Title but no name	Misspellings of common words
Excessive weight	Oily stains, discolorations
Handwritten address	No return address
Strange odor	Visual distractions
Lopsided or uneven envelope	Protruding wire / aluminum foil
Ticking Sound	"Personal" or "Confidential"

Is the recipient / victim a likely target of attack?

MAILED FROM A FOREIGN COUNTRY — EXCESSIVE OR NO POSTAGE

NO RETURN ADDRESS

RESTRICTIVE MARKINGS

STRANGE ODOR

LOPSIDED PACKAGE

RIGID OR BULKY ENVELOPE

ADDRESS:
- BADLY TYPED OR WRITTEN
- MISSPELLED
- TITLE WITH NO NAME
- WRONG TITLE WITH NAME

PRECAUTIONS

1. Never accept mail, especially packages, while in a foreign country.

2. Make sure family members and clerical staff know to refuse all unexpected mail at home or office.

3. Remember - IT MAY BE A BOMB - Treat it as suspect.

PROTRUDING WIRES

OILY STAINS ON WRAPPER

FOR MORE INFORMATION ON BOMB SECURITY
OR BOMB THREAT, CONTACT YOUR LOCAL ATF OFFICE

Terror

Fatal / Multi-Vehicle Accident

ENSURE OFFICER SAFETY— Use Universal Precautions (see page 80)

1. **Scene Security and Safety**
   - ✓ Protection of valuables
2. **Verification of Death - Who Determined**
   - ✓ Medical examiner
   - ✓ EMS
3. **Identification of All Parties and Witnesses Involved**
4. **Determine If Crime Has Been Committed**
   - ✓ Advise of rights
   - ✓ Position of occupants
   - ✓ Safety restraints used?
5. **Notification of Accident Reconstructionist**
   - ✓ Mark vehicle locations
6. **Preservation or Seizure of Physical Evidence**
   - ✓ Hair / blood
   - ✓ Clothes / fibers
   - ✓ Open containers
7. **Two (2) Blood / Urine Samples from Surviving Driver**
   - ✓ One (I) hour apart
8. **Storage of Vehicles if Needed For Reconstructionist**
   - ✓ Processing of vehicle
   - ✓ Crime lab
9. **Additional Considerations**
   - ✓ Search warrant
   - ✓ Review any video coverage of incident
   - ✓ Inspect vehicles mechanically
   - ✓ Provide landing zone for helicopter (see page 60)

Fire & Arson Investigation

ENSURE OFFICER SAFETY

1 Initial Response
   ✓ Observe fire & scene conditions
     • Location & condition of victims / witnesses
   ✓ Be aware of persons / vehicle leaving the scene
2 Exercise Scene Safety
   ✓ Evaluate the scene for safety hazards
   ✓ Establish safety / hazard zones
   ✓ Communicate hazards to other responders
   ✓ Approach in a manner to reduce risk to officer(s)

WARNING: Beware of incendiary or explosive devices! Do not touch any suspected incendiary or explosive device. Evacuate the area, and request the services of personnel trained in the removal of such items.

1 Preserve the Fire Scene
   ✓ Observe & mentally note evidence
   ✓ Recognize threats to evidence
   ✓ Protect evidence
2 Establish Security & Control
   ✓ Set up a security perimeter
   ✓ Control access into the scene
   ✓ Initiate documentation of the scene
     • Photograph / videotape scene
3 Coordinate Activities
   ✓ Establish command post / implement ICS, see page 33
   ✓ Establish staging area(s)
   ✓ Request additional resources
4 Evaluating the Scene
   ✓ Define the extent of the scene
   ✓ Identify & interview witnesses at the scene

5 Processing Evidence at the Scene
- ✓ Identify, collect, and preserve evidence
- ✓ Establish & maintain the chain of custody

Helicopter Landing Zones

ENSURE OFFICER SAFETY:
- ▼ Wear fastened helmet, eye & ear protection
- ▼ Protect self and patient from rotorwash

1 Activation
- ✓ Location of incident (cross streets), map coordinates, major landmarks, lakes, rivers, GPS coordinates
- ✓ Landing Zone (LZ) information
- ✓ LZ Scene Coordinator 's name / # (assign one person)
- ✓ Patient information (number, ages, condition)
- ✓ Inform if hazardous materials are involved
- ✓ Inform if OC / CS / CN or other tactical agents used
- ✓ Specify scene radio frequency

2 Landing Zone
- ✓ LZ should be 100' x 100'
- ✓ Clear of overhead wires and obstructions
- ✓ Flat, level, firm surface, free of debris
- ✓ If possible, water down dry dirt or sand
- ✓ Mark with strobes, cones, or flares
- ✓ Flares should be secured to the ground
- ✓ If HazMat select LZ upwind, 1 mile from HazMat, and NOT in low lying area

3 Provide LZ Information to Pilot
- ✓ Exact LZ location including GPS coordinates
- ✓ LZ markings & obstructions, wind speed & direction
- ✓ LZ coordinator's location (in front if possible)

LANDING ZONE SAFETY

- Report all hazards (trees, wires, etc.) to flight crew
- Do not radio aircraft during last 30 seconds before landing except to report an immediate hazard
- If so, state "ABORT" or "GO AROUND"
- Never shine lights at the aircraft
- Never approach aircraft from the rear
- If landing on a slope — approach from downhill side
- The pilot cannot see wires — emphasize the exact location and height of wires within 300' of LZ
- Keep all persons out of LZ during landing and take-off

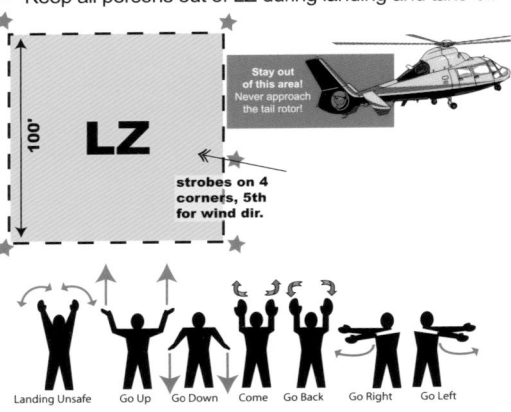

Stay out of this area! Never approach the tail rotor!

LZ

100'

strobes on 4 corners, 5th for wind dir.

Landing Unsafe   Go Up   Go Down   Come   Go Back   Go Right   Go Left

NOTE: Consider placing the helicopter on "Standby" to reduce lift-off time. Remember that it may not be able to fly in certain conditions: fog, freezing rain, snow, thunderstorms. The pilot makes the final decision whether to fly or not.

Your Aeromedical Service #

2 Response Recommendations:
- ✓ Command post should be located away from areas where improvised secondary devices may be placed, e.g., mailboxes, trash cans, etc.
- ✓ Stage incoming units:
  - Away from line of sight of target area.
  - Away from buildings with large amounts of glass.
  - In such a way as to utilize distant structural and / or natural barriers to assist with protection.

3 Unexploded Device / Pre-Blast Operations:
- ✓ Isolate / deny entry

4 Attempt to identify device characteristics:
- ✓ Type of threat
- ✓ Location / Time
- ✓ Package / Device
- ✓ Associated history

WARNING: Use extreme caution if caller indicates time for detonation. It is very possible that the device will activate prior to the announced time.

- ✓ Secure perimeter based on the size of device (see Stand-Off Chart on page 124)
- ✓ Discontinue use of all radios, Mobile Data Terminals (MDT) and cell phones in accordance with local protocol

5 Evaluate scene conditions:
- ✓ Potential number of affected people
- ✓ Exposure problems
- ✓ Potential hazards: utilities, structures, fires, chemicals, etc.
- ✓ Water supply
- ✓ Evaluate available resources (, HazMat, Technical Rescue, etc.)
- ✓ Review pre-plans for affected buildings

6 Exploded Device / Post-Blast Operation:
- ✓ Stage incoming units at a greater distance

assistance
- ✓ HazMat personnel in chemical PPE may be used for rescue, recon, and agent identification
- ✓ Nonsymptomatic patients should be decontaminated and then forwarded to
  - • Use soap-and-water decon

EXPLOSIVES

ENSURE RESPONDER SAFETY

1 General Information
  - ✓ Explosive devices may be designed to disseminate chemical, biological or radiological agents
  - ✓ Explosives may produce secondary hazards such as unstable structures, damaged utilities, hanging debris, void spaces and other physical hazards
  - ✓ Devices may contain anti-personnel features such as nails, shrapnel, fragmentation design or other material
  - ✓ Outward warning signs:
    - • Oral or written threats
    - • Container / vehicle / people that appear out of place
    - • Devices attached to compressed gas cylinders, flammable, liquid containers, bulk storage containers (dirty bomb)
    - • Oversized packages with oily stains, chemical odors, excessive postage, protruding wires, excessive binding, no return address, etc.
  - ✓ NAERGs #112 and 114 provide additional information

WARNING: Always be alert for multiple devices

Terror

- Blister agents (Guide #153)
- Blood agents (Guides #117, 119, 125)
- Choking agents (Guides #124, 125)
- Irritant agents (riot control) (Guides #153, 159)

2 Response Recommendations

✓ Approach from uphill and upwind
✓ Note: Victims exposed to chemical agents require immediate removal of clothing, gross decontamination and definitive medical care.
✓ Stage at a safe distance away from the site
✓ Secure and isolate the area / deny entry
✓ Complete a hazard and risk assessment to determine if it is acceptable to commit responders to the site
✓ Be aware of larger secondary chemical devices
✓ Personal in structural PPE / SCBA may enter the hot zone near the perimeter (outside areas of high concentration) to perform lifesaving functions
✓ Move ambulatory patients away from the area of highest concentration or source
✓ Confine all contaminated and exposed victims to a restricted / isolated area at the outer edge of the hot zone
✓ Symptomatic patients should be segregated into one area and asymptomatic patients should be placed in another area
✓ Establish an outer perimeter to completely secure scene
✓ If agent is known or suspected, notify / hospitals so sufficient quantities of antidotes can be obtained
✓ Hospitals should be notified immediately that contaminated victims of the attack may arrive or self-present at the hospital
✓ Begin emergency gross decontamination procedures starting with the most severe,

ENSURE OFFICER SAFETY

1 General Information
   ✓ A majority of chemicals exist as liquids and must
     be aerosolized or vaporized for maximum
     exposure potential. If there is no dissemination
     device, there will not be as large a hot zone.
   ✓ Victims' signs and symptoms of hazardous
     substance exposure:
     • Are there unconscious victims with minimal or no
       trauma?
     • Are there victims exhibiting:

SLUDGE-M	DUMBELS
Salivation	Diarrhea
Lacrimation	Urination
Urination	Miosis
Defecation	Broncho constriction
Gastointestinal problems	Emesis
Emesis	Lacrimation
Miosis	Salivation

     • Is there blistering, reddening, discoloration,
       irritation of skin?
     • Are victims having difficulty breathing?
   ✓ Look for physical indicators and other outward
     warning sign:
     • Medical mass casualty / fatality with minimal or
       no trauma
     • Responder casualties
     • Dead animals and vegetation
     • Unusual odors, color of smoke, vapor clouds
   ✓ DOT-ERGs provide additional information:
     • Nerve agents (Guide #153)

Terror

Letter	Police	Military
A	Adam	Alpha
B	Boy	Bravo
C	Charles	Charlie
D	David	Delta
E	Edward	Echo
F	Frank	Foxtrot
G	George	Golf
H	Henry	Hotel
I	Ida	India
J	John	Juliet
K	King	Kilo
L	Lincoln	Lima
M	Mary	Mike
N	Nora	November
O	Ocean	Oscar
P	Paul	Papa
Q	Queen	Quebec
R	Robert	Romeo
S	Sand	Sierra
T	Tom	Tango
U	Union	Uniform
V	Victor	Victor
W	William	Whiskey
X	X-ray	X-ray
Y	Yellow	Yankee
Z	Zebra	Zulu

Six Levels of Force

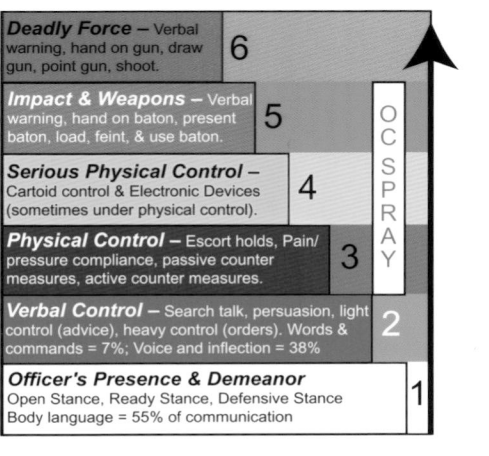

Deadly Force – Verbal warning, hand on gun, draw gun, point gun, shoot. **6**

Impact & Weapons – Verbal warning, hand on baton, present baton, load, feint, & use baton. **5**

Serious Physical Control – Cartoid control & Electronic Devices (sometimes under physical control). **4**

Physical Control – Escort holds, Pain/pressure compliance, passive counter measures, active counter measures. **3**

Verbal Control – Search talk, persuasion, light control (advice), heavy control (orders). Words & commands = 7%; Voice and inflection = 38% **2**

Officer's Presence & Demeanor Open Stance, Ready Stance, Defensive Stance Body language = 55% of communication **1**

O C S P R A Y

Sudden escalation of threats, aggression, or resistance by suspects may preclude the use of lesser levels of force or control by officers. The decision to employ any given level of force must be based solely on the facts known to, or reasonably believed, by officers at the time the action is taken. *Prepare report to justify level of force used.* Include factors which may effect the "reasonableness" of the level of force:

- Officer's age
- Officer's size
- Relative strength of officer
- <u>Skill level of the officer. etc.</u>

Speed Enforcement

NOTE: ALWAYS ENSURE OFFICER SAFETY

The officer should choose a location to initiate the traffic stop that will provide, as much as possible, a safe environment for the driver and law enforcement officer.

1 Tracking History
- ✓ The most essential component of speed enforcement & courtroom testimony
- ✓ Visual observation & estimation
- ✓ Audio confirmation
- ✓ Device corroboration

2 Visual Observation
- ✓ Target identification
- ✓ Estimation of target speed
- ✓ Estimation of distance to target
- ✓ Check environment

3 Audio Confirmation
- ✓ Pitch of audio
- ✓ Clarity of audio

Vehicle Stopping Distances

Speed	Stopping Distances	
	Dry Pavement	**Wet Pavement**
25 m.p.h.	61 ft.	65 ft.
30 m.p.h.	79 ft.	85 ft.
35 m.p.h.	98 ft.	107 ft.
40 m.p.h.	120 ft.	131 ft.
45 m.p.h.	144 ft.	157 ft.
50 m.p.h.	169 ft.	186 ft.
55 m.p.h.	197 ft.	217 ft.
60 m.p.h.	226 ft.	250 ft.
65 m.p.h.	258 ft.	286 ft.
70 m.p.h.	291 ft.	324 ft.
75 m.p.h.	326 ft.	364 ft.
80 m.p.h.	363 ft.	406 ft.
85 m.p.h.	402 ft.	451 ft.
90 m.p.h.	443 ft.	498 ft.
95 m.p.h.	486 ft.	547 ft.
100 m.p.h.	531 ft.	598 ft.

Assumptions

1 Stopping Distance = distance covered from hazard recognition until vehicle is stopped (without skidding)
2 Average passenger vehicle
3 Reaction time of 1.0 second
4 Deceleration Rates:
   ❏ Dry Pavement=28.0 ft/second^2
   ❏ Wet Pavement=23.9 ft/second^2

Truck Stopping Distances

Speed	Reaction/Braking Distance	Stopping Distance
30m.p.h.	33/67 ft.	100 ft.
40m.p.h.	44/125 ft.	169 ft.
55m.p.h.	60/275 ft.	335 ft.
60m.p.h.	66/360 ft.	426 ft.
65m.p.h.	71/454 ft.	525 ft.

Estimates are for 80,000 lb., loaded tractor-trailer traveling on a dry, level road surface.

Two-Plate Requirement

The following states require both a front and rear license plate to be displayed:

Alaska	Maryland	Ohio
California	Minnesota	Oregon
Colorado	Missouri	Rhode Island
Connecticut	Montana	South Dakota
District of Columbia	Nebraska	Texas
Hawaii	Nevada	Utah
Idaho	New Hampshire	Virginia
Illinois	New Jersey	Washington
Iowa	New York	Wisconsin
Maine	North Dakota	Wyoming

High Risk Traffic Stop Procedure

1 Initial Tactics
- ✓ Radio vehicle plate, description, occupant info
- ✓ Communicate high-risk stop decision to other units
- ✓ Pre-plan location for stop
- ✓ Initiate stop & position units (Contact / Cover)

2 Initial Instructions (Contact Officer)
- ✓ Assume position of cover
- ✓ Announce:
  - "Turn off engine"
  - "Don't move"
  - "Throw keys out window"
  - "Driver / Passenger: put your hands against windshield"
  - "Backseat: put hands on back of front seat"
- ✓ Approach in a manner to reduce risk to officer(s)

3 Removal of Occupants (Contact Officer)
- ✓ Announce (begin with driver)
  - "Reach your hand out the window and open the door from the outside"
  - "Step out of the car"
  - "Put your hands up"
  - "Put your hands behind your head"
  - "Kick the door shut"

4 Control (Contact Officer)
- ✓ Maintain cover & announce:
  - "With your hands up, walk backwards toward the sound of my voice" (have subject move to left / right as necessary)
- ✓ When positioned correctly instruct subject to kneel
  - "Lie flat on your front w/arms out to sides"
  - "Palms up"
  - "Cross your feet at the ankles"

5 Custody From Prone Position (Cover Officer)
- ✓ Instruct to turn head away from custody officer

6 Clear Vehicle (Contact & Cover)
- ✓ "You in vehicle — we know you are there — sit up now"
- ✓ Clear vehicle — maximize officer safety

High Risk Traffic Stop Positioning

1 Contact Officer:
- ✓ Responsible for business of stop
- ✓ Communicates with occupants

2 Cover Officer:
- ✓ Provides cover for contact officer
- ✓ Takes occupants into custody

3 Custody Location:
- ✓ Location where occupants are taken into custody
- ✓ Location may be moved to ensure officer safety

4 Additional Cover Officers:
- ✓ Patrol units behind primary units
- ✓ Assume position of cover at primary units

Unknown Risk Traffic Stop

1 Initial Tactics
- ✓ Check "want" status on vehicle plate
- ✓ Pre-plan location of stop
- ✓ Radio vehicle plate & location of stop
- ✓ Activate overhead lights & effect vehicle stop
- ✓ Position patrol unit for maximum cover
- ✓ Observe actions of vehicle occupants
- ✓ Illuminate interior of occupant's vehicle

2 Approach & Contact
- ✓ Maintain tactical advantage
- ✓ Pre-plan escape route(s) & positions of cover

✓ Check to see if trunk lid is latched
✓ Contact driver - maintain tactical position
3 Obtain Necessary Information for Contact
4 Conduct State / NCIC / Driving Status Inquiry
5 Citation / Warning / Search, etc.
6 Advise Dispatch You Are Clear From The Stop

DUI Investigation

ENSURE OFFICER SAFETY

1 Vehicle in Motion
✓ Initial observation
✓ Observation of stop
2 Personal Contact
✓ Observation of driver
✓ Statements
✓ Observation of exit
3 Pre-Arrest Screening
✓ Horizontal Gaze Nystagmus
✓ Walk and Turn
✓ One Leg Stand
✓ Other Field Sobriety Tests
4 General Observations
✓ Speech
✓ Attitude
✓ Breath odors
✓ Color of face
✓ Eyes
✓ Pupils
✓ Clothing
✓ Unusual actions
5 Arrest Decision

ENSURE OFFICER SAFETY

1 Audio / Video Record:
- ✓ Name
- ✓ Badge
- ✓ Date
- ✓ Time Location
- ✓ Plate
- ✓ Driver Info

2 Advise subject conversation is being recorded

3 Request subject to perform field sobriety tests

4 Ask:
- ☐ "Are you sick or injured?"
- ☐ "Do you have diabetes?"
- ☐ "Are you hypoglycemic?"
- ☐ "Do you have any head / neck / back / leg injuries?"
- ☐ "How much education have you had?"
- ☐ "Do you have speech problems?"
- ☐ "Do you have any hearing problems?"
- ☐ "Do you have any balance problems?"
- ☐ "Is this your car?"
- ☐ "Were you driving?"
- ☐ "Where were you going?"

5 Advise:
- ☐ "Each test will be demonstrated"
- ☐ "Do not begin until you are told to do so"
- ☐ "Do you understand the instructions?"

Pre-Arrest Screening — Standard Tests

Horizontal Gaze Nystagmus (HGN)
(4 / 6 Clues — 77% reliable)

RECITE
- I am going to check your eyes (Please remove your glasses).
- Keep your head still and follow the stimulus with your eyes only.
- Do not move your head.
- Do you understand the instructions?

CHECK

Corrective lens	☐ None	☐ Glasses
Contact lens	☐ Hard	☐ Soft
Eye appearance	☐ Normal	☐ Bloodshot
	☐ Glassy	☐ Watery
Blindness	☐ Right	☐ Left
Tracking	☐ Equal	☐ Unequal
Pupil Size	☐ Equal	☐ Unequal
Resting HGN	☐ Yes	☐ No
Follow stimulus	☐ Yes	☐ No
Eyelids	☐ Normal	☐ Droopy

	Right		Left
Lack of Smooth Pursuit	☐		☐
Distinct nystagmus at maximum deviation	☐		☐
Onset of nystagmus prior to 45 degrees	☐		☐

Vertical Nystagmus	☐	**Yes**	☐ **No**

TOTAL CLUES _____

RECITE

- Stand with your heels together and your arms at your side. (Demonstrate).
- Do not begin the test until I tell you to.
- Do you understand?
- When I tell you to, I want you to raise one leg, either leg, approximately six inches off the ground, foot pointed out. Keep both legs straight and keep your eyes on the elevated foot.
- While holding that position, count out loud; one thousand and one, one thousand and two, one thousand and three, and so forth until told to stop. (Demonstrate raised leg and count)
- Do you understand the instructions?
- You may begin the test.

SCORE

- ❑ Sways while balancing
- ❑ Uses arms for balance
- ❑ Hopping
- ❑ Puts foot down

_____ TOTAL Clues

Cannot Do Test (explain): _____
_____
_____

WALK & TURN (WAT)
(2 / 8 Clues - 68% reliable)

RECITE

- Put your left foot on the line and put your right foot in front of it with your right heel touching your left toe. Keep your hands at your side. (Demonstrate).
- Do not start until I tell you to.
- Do you understand the directions?

- When I tell you to begin, take nine heel-to-toe steps on the line, turn around keeping one foot on the line, and return nine heel-to-toe steps. (Demonstrate heel-to-toe; three steps is sufficient).
- On the ninth step, keep the front foot on the line and turn by taking several small steps with the other foot. (Demonstrate turn)
- While Walking, watch your feet at all times, keep arms at side, count steps out loud. Once you begin, do not stop until test is completed.
- Do you understand the directions?
- You may begin the test.

SCORE

- ❏ Cannot keep balance during instructions
- ❏ Starts walking before instructions are finished
- ❏ Stops walking to steady self
- ❏ Steps off line

_____TOTAL Clues

	First Nine	Second Nine
Stops walking	1-2-3-4-5-6-7-8-9	1-2-3-4-5-6-7-8-9
Misses heel-to-toe	1-2-3-4-5-6-7-8-9	1-2-3-4-5-6-7-8-9
Steps off line	1-2-3-4-5-6-7-8-9	1-2-3-4-5-6-7-8-9
Raises arms	1-2-3-4-5-6-7-8-9	1-2-3-4-5-6-7-8-9
Improper turn	1-2-3-4-5-6-7-8-9	1-2-3-4-5-6-7-8-9
Actual Steps Taken		
Cannot do test		

Modified Attention Romberg
  Balance - Eyes Closed
  • Front / Back Sway
  • Side-to-Side Sway
  • Circular Sway

Modified Finger to Nose
  Balance - Eyes Closed
  • Front / Back Sway
  • Side-to-Side Sway
  • Circular Sway

Finger Count

1-2-3-4	4-3-2-1
Missed Finger	Missed Finger
Missed Counting	Missed Counting
1-2-3-4	4-3-2-1
Missed Finger	Missed Finger
Missed Counting	Missed Counting

Alphabet
A B C D E F G H I J K L M N O P Q R S T U V W X Y Z

Backwards Count From 100
99 98 97 96 95 94 93 92 91 90 89 88 87 86 85 84 83
82 81 80 79 78 77 76

Romberg Internal Clock

RECITE
• Stand with feet together
• Arms at side
• Watch me and listen while I give you instructions
• Tilt head back slightly, close eyes
• Estimate 30 seconds
• Open eyes, tilt head forward and say stop
• How much time was that?

Estimated 30 Seconds = _____

OTHER DATA

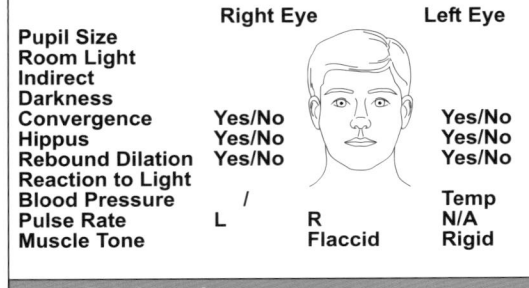

	Right Eye	Left Eye
Pupil Size		
Room Light		
Indirect		
Darkness		
Convergence	Yes/No	Yes/No
Hippus	Yes/No	Yes/No
Rebound Dilation	Yes/No	Yes/No
Reaction to Light		
Blood Pressure	/	Temp
Pulse Rate	L R	N/A
Muscle Tone	Flaccid	Rigid

Post-Test Interview

1 Advise subject tests are over
2 Recite Miranda Warning (see page 2)
3 "Do you feel the effects of the alcohol you have consumed?"
4 "Do you feel intoxicated?"
5 "Do you feel the alcohol has influenced your ability to drive?"

Alcohol/Drug Detection Guide

Driver Observations

Chances in 100 of nighttime driver with BAC equal to or greater than 0.10%

Driver Error	%
Turning with wide radius	65
Straddling center or lane marker	65
Appearing to be drunk	60
Almost striking object or vehicle	60
Weaving	60
Driving on other than designated road	55
Swerving	55
Slow speed (↑10 m.p.h. below posted speed)	50
Following too closely	50
Drifting	50
Tires on center or lane marker	45
Braking erratically	45
Driving into opposing / crossing traffic	45
Signaling inconsistent with actions	40
Slow response to traffic signals	40
Stopping inappropriately	35
Turning abruptly or illegally	35
Accelerating or decelerating rapidly	30
Headlights off	30

If two (2) or more clues are observed — add 10 to the larger value

On Friday & Saturday from 21:00 to 02:00 ONE in SEVEN Drivers have a BAC of 0.10% or Greater

Suspect Observations

Appearance
Clean	Orderly	Disarranged	Bloody
Vomit	Urine		

Attitude
Agitated	Cooperative	Polite	Disinterested
Drowsy	Confused	Mood Swings	Memory Loss
Hallucinating	Laughing	Uninhibited	Disoriented
Stuporous	Fumbling	Anxious	Restless

Speech
None	Incoherent	Slow	Thick/Slurred
Talkative	Rapid	Repetitive	

Face
Normal	Flushed	Pale	Other

Eyes
Normal	Watery	Bloodshot	Pink/Red

Actions
Flaccid	Rigid	Nodding	Drooping Lids
Raspy Voice	Dry Mouth	Itching Face	Body Tremors
Runny Nose	Track Marks	Perspiring	Paraphernalia
Nasal Redness	Grinding Teeth (Bruxism)		

Pupil Gauge

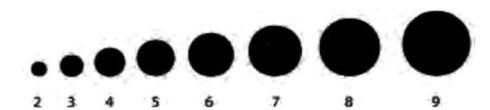

2   3   4   5   6   7   8   9

Blood Alcohol Content

Number of drinks by body weight = BAC. Limit varies by state.

	100	120	140	160	180	200	220	240
1	.04	.04	.03	.03	.02	.02	.02	.02
2	.08	.06	.05	.05	.04	.04	.03	.03
3	.11	.09	.08	.07	.07	.06	.05	.05
4	.15	.12	.11	.09	.08	.08	.07	.06
5	.19	.16	.13	.12	.11	.09	.09	.08
6	.23	.19	.16	.14	.13	.11	.10	.09
7	.26	.22	.19	.16	.15	.13	.12	.11
8	.30	.25	.21	.19	.17	.15	.14	.13
9	.34	.28	.24	.21	.19	.17	.15	.14
10	.38	.31	.27	.23	.21	.19	.17	.16

Drug Impairment Recognition

	HGN	VGN	Pupil Size
CNS Depressant	Present	Present (high dose*)	Normal[1]
CNS Stimulant	None	None	Dilated
Hallucinogens	None	None	Dilated
PCP	Present	Present	
Narcotics	None	None	Constricted
Inhalants	Present	Present (high dose*)	Normal[2]
Cannabis	None	None	Dilated[3]

[1] Soma® & Quaalude® usually dilate
[2] Normal, but may be dilated
[3] Possibly normal

High dose means a high dosage for that particular individual.

Controlled Substances & Indicators

Schedule I: Substances include: heroin, LSD, marijuana, and methaqualone, MDMA (ecstasy), GHB, and Nexus.

Schedule II: Substances include: morphine, PCP, cocaine, methadone, and methamphetamine.

Schedule III: Substances include: anabolic steroids, rohypnol, ketamine, codeine and hydrocodone with aspirin or Tylenol®, and some barbiturates.

Schedule IV: Substances include: Darvon®, Talwin®, Equanil®, Valium® and Xanax®.

Schedule V: Substances include: Penicillin, and over-the-counter cough medicines with codeine.

OTC (not controlled): Including: Tylenol®, Ibuprofen, etc.

Cannabis

Marijuana and other Cannabis products impair the attention process. Ability to perform divided-attention tasks diminishes under the influence of Cannabis.
Examples: Marijuana; Hashish; Hash Oil.
Indicators: Very bloodshot eyes; body tremors; eyelid tremors; odor of marijuana; marijuana debris in mouth; increased appetite; disoriented; relaxed inhibitions; difficulty in dividing attention.
Eye Indicators: No nystagmus present; pupil size will be near normal or slightly dilated.
Method of Administration: Smoked; oral.
Overdose Signs: Fatigue; paranoia.

Central Nervous System Depressants

CNS Depressants slow down the operations of the brain. They depress heartbeat, blood pressure, and respiration.

Examples: Alcohol; barbiturates; anti-anxiety tranquilizers (e.g., Valium®, Librium®); many others.

Indicators: "Drunken" behavior; sluggish; uncoordinated; disoriented; drowsy; thick, slurred speech; gait ataxia; droopy eyes.

Eye Indicators: HGN usually present; vertical nystagmus possible; pupil size usually normal (except methaqualone - dilated).

Method of Administration: Oral; injected.

Overdose Signs: Shallow breathing; cold, clammy skin; dilated pupils; rapid, weak pulse; coma.

With methaqualone, Quaalude®, and alcohol, pulse may elevate. Soma® and Quaalude dilate pupils.

Central Nervous System Stimulants

CNS Stimulants accelerate the heart and respiratory rate, elevate blood pressure, and "speed up" the body.

Examples: Cocaine; amphetamines (e.g., methamphetamine, dextroamphetamine, amphetamine sulfate, etc.).

Indicators: Restlessness; talkative; excitation; euphoria; exaggerated reflexes; grinding teeth (bruxism); redness to nasal area (if "snorting"); runny nose; body tremors; loss of appetite; dry mouth, irritability.

Eye Indicators: No nystagmus present; pupils dilated.

Method of Administration: Insufflation (snorting); smoked; injected.

Overdose Signs: Agitation; increased body temperature.

Hallucinogens

Hallucinogens cause hallucinations, i.e., they cause the user to perceive things differently from the way they really are.

Examples: Peyote (derives from cactus); psilocybin (derives from mushrooms); LSD; MDA; many others.

Indicators: Hallucinations; dazed appearance; body tremors; uncoordinated; perspiring; disorientation; paranoia; difficulty in speech; nausea; perspiring; memory loss; flashbacks.

Eye Indicators: No nystagmus present; pupils dilated.

Method of Administration: Oral; insufflation; smoked; injected; transdermal (skin);

Overdose Signs: Long intense "trip".

Inhalants

Some inhalants include psycho-active chemicals that produce a variety of effects. Others exert their major effect by blocking the passage of oxygen to the brain.

Examples: Volatile substances (glue, paint, gasoline); Aerosols (hair spray, insecticides); anesthetics (nitrous oxide, ether, chloroform).

Indicators: Disorientation; confusion; slurred speech; nausea; residue on face, hands, clothing; odor of substance; bloodshot, watery eyes; lack of muscle control; flushed face; intense headache; non-communicative.

Eye Indicators: HGN usually present; vertical nystagmus possible; pupil size usually normal.

Method of Administration: Insufflation (snorting).

Overdose Signs: Coma

Narcotic Analgesics

Narcotic analgesics are highly addictive pain control medications which will produce withdrawal signs and symptoms when the drug is stopped after chronic administration.

Examples: Morphine; heroin; codeine; demerol; methadone; many other opium derivatives and synthetic opiates.

Indicators: "On the nod"; droopy eyelids (ptosis); depressed reflexes; dry mouth; facial itching; low, raspy speech; fresh puncture marks; euphoria; track marks.

Eye Indicators: No nystagmus present; pupils severely constricted.

Method of Administration: Injected; oral; smoked; insufflation (snorting).

Overdose Signs: Slow shallow breathing; cool, clammy skin; coma; convulsions.

PCP

PCP is a powerful anesthetic. However, it also causes bizarre and often violent behavior.

Examples: PCP; Angel Dust.

Indicators: Perspiration; repetitive speech; confusion; possibly violent and combative; blank stare; incomplete verbal responses; muscle rigidity; warm to the touch; increased pain threshold; cyclic behavior; chemical odor; "moon walking".

Eye Indicators: HGN present with very early onset and very distinct jerking; vertical nystagmus present; resting nystagmus possible; pupil size is usually normal.

Method of Administration: Smoked; oral; insufflation (snorting) injected; eye drops.

Overdose Signs: Long, intense "trip".

Party Drugs

MDMA (3, 4-methylenedioxymethamphetamine)
Street Names: Ecstasy, XTC, E, X, and Adam

Ketamine
Street Names: K, Special K, and Cat Valium

GHB
Street Names: Liquid Ecstasy, Soap, Easy Lay, Boy, Grievous Bodily Harm, Liquid X, and Goop

Rohypnol (Flunitrazepam)
Street Names: Roofies, Rophies, Roche, Forget-me Pill, Circles, Mexican Valium, Rib, Roach-2, Roopies, Rope, Ropies, Ruffies, and Roaches

Nexus (2-(4-Bromo-2,5-dimethoxy-phenyl)-ethylamine)
Street Names: Venus, Bromo, Nexus, 2CB, Spectrum, BDMPEA, Toonies, and MFT

EXAMPLE: The following is an outline for a typical police report

2 Summary
- ✓ Brief synopsis of incident
- ✓ What crime / incident was investigated
- ✓ What was the outcome or disposition of investigation

3 Mentioned
- ✓ List all persons mentioned in report
- ✓ List the role of each, i.e., suspect, witness, victim
- ✓ Document name, DOB, address, phone, etc.

4 Action Taken
- ✓ Describe what you saw, heard, and did at the scene
- ✓ Be specific — use factual statements

5 Victim / Witness / Subject Statement(s)
- ✓ State what they told you they had seen, done, heard
- ✓ Paraphrase most of the statements
- ✓ Consider written / taped statements

6 Investigation of the Scene
- ✓ Describe investigation of evidence
- ✓ Describe circumstances of finding evidence
- ✓ Identify significance of evidence

7 Evidentiary Exhibits
- ✓ Document chain of custody
- ✓ Maintain evidence log
- ✓ Document evidence — search warrants, subpoenas

8 Disposition
- ✓ Identify disposition of the investigation / arrest
- ✓ Identify any follow-up activities

Scouting Locations

ENSURE OFFICER SAFETY

1 Structure
- ✓ Type: business, residence, multi-story
- ✓ Size & type of windows (casement, sliding, picture)
- ✓ Are windows barred, covered with storm windows
- ✓ Size & type of doors (sliding, hollow, French, etc.)
- ✓ Are doors barred and / or protected by storm door
- ✓ Do doors open in or out
- ✓ Utility shut-off locations (water, gas, power, phone)
- ✓ Location of bathrooms (vent pipes, windows, etc.)
- ✓ Exterior lighting locations

2 Planning
- ✓ Location from which to create diversion
- ✓ Location from which to make announcements
- ✓ Best location to introduce chemical agents
- ✓ General descriptions of adjacent residences / buildings

3 Potential Hazards
- ✓ Dogs, fences, holes in ground, clotheslines, etc.
- ✓ Locations that may require evacuation
- ✓ Locations of possible hostile neighbors

4 Recommendations
- ✓ Positions (covered & concealed) for team members
- ✓ Position for entry team
- ✓ Evacuation route for injured team members
- ✓ Exit point(s) for suspect(s) in the event of surrender

5 Target Identification
- ✓ Sides: alphabetical & clockwise from front
- ✓ Floors: numerical beginning on ground floor
- ✓ Corners: "AB corner" (front left) "CD corner" (rear right) etc.

Seizure of Electronic Evidence

ENSURE OFFICER SAFETY

1 Determine The Computer's Role
- ✓ Is the computer contraband or fruits of the crime?
- ✓ Is the computer system a tool of the offense?
- ✓ Is the computer system instrumental to the offense and a storage device for evidence?

2 Essential Information
- ✓ Is there probable cause to seize hardware?
- ✓ Is there probable cause to seize software?
- ✓ Is there probable cause to seize data?

3 Preparing For the Search and / or Seizure
- ✓ Use appropriate collection techniques so as not to alter or destroy evidence
- ✓ Forensic examination of the system completed by expert personnel

4 Conducting the Search and / or Seizure
- ✓ Preserve area for potential fingerprints
- ✓ Immediately restrict access to computer(s)
  - Isolate from phone lines

5 Secure the Computer as Evidence
- ✓ If computer is "OFF"— DO NOT TURN "ON"
- ✓ If stand-alone (non-networked) computer is "ON"
  - Consult computer specialist
- ✓ If computer specialist is not available
  - Photograph screen, disconnect from power sources, unplug from wall AND back of computer
  - Place evidence tape on each drive slot
  - Photograph / diagram & label back of computer components with existing connections
  - Package components & transport / store as fragile cargo
  - Keep away from magnets, radio transmitters or other hostile environments

70

- ✓ If networked or business computer, consult a computer specialist—pulling the cord could cause severe damage

6 Other Electronic Storage Devices
- ✓ Wireless telephones, pagers, fax machine, caller ID device, smart cards

Vehicle Pursuit

ENSURE OFFICER SAFETY — DOES THE GRAVITY OF THE CRIME JUSTIFY THE PURSUIT?

1 Radio
- ✓ Unit ID number
- ✓ Location & direction of travel
- ✓ Description of vehicle & suspect
- ✓ Description & number of occupants
- ✓ Reason for pursuit
- ✓ Clear radio frequency

2 Update
- ✓ Direction change / action & speed of vehicle

3 Action
- ✓ Check for stolen
- ✓ Reduce speed & back off
- ✓ Give suspect opportunity to stop
- ✓ Limit number of chase vehicles
- ✓ Use overhead lights & siren

4 Location / Safety of Pursuit
- ✓ Rural vs. populated area
- ✓ Hazard to community
- ✓ Time of day / day of week
- ✓ Vehicle / pedestrian traffic
- ✓ Road / weather / driver / vehicle conditions

5 Consider
- ✓ Can suspect be identified at a later date
- ✓ Officer's experience
- ✓ Type of patrol unit - marked / unmarked

- ✓ Use of aircraft
- ✓ Jurisdiction — interstate / multi-county
- ✓ Block access roadways — protection of public

6 **Is gravity of crime such that vehicle must be stopped?**
   - ✓ Can vehicle be followed?

7 **Pursued Driver Stopped**
   - ✓ High-risk vehicle stop
   - ✓ Prepare report justifying pursuit
   - ✓ Follow-up critique with officers / agencies

Notes

The Spanish language consists of the same letters as the English alphabet and the four (4) additional characters: CH, LL, N, and RR.

▼ **CH:** Is pronounced like the "ch" in "church" at all times; LL: Like the English consonant "Y";
▼ **N:** Like the "ny" in "canyon";
▼ **RR:** Very strongly trilled, with the front top portion of the tongue on the roof of the mouth behind the teeth.
▼ **"K" and "W"** appear only in foreign words and are pronounced in the same way as in the foreign word.
▼ In Spanish, the letter "**H**" is always silent.
▼ The Letter "**J**" is pronounced like the English "h" in "house" Spanish consonants do not differ significantly from those found in English.

Spanish vowels maintain the following pronunciations at all times:

▼ **A:** Sounds like the "a" in "father";
▼ **E:** Sounds like the "e" in "they";
▼ **I:** Sounds like the "i" in "police";
▼ **O:** Sounds like the "o" in "";
▼ **U:** Sounds like the "u" in "rude";
▼ **QU:** Sounds like the "c" in "coal".

MIRANDA WARNING

Es mi deber informaril que antes de hacer una declaracion:

- Usted tiene el derecho de quedarse callado.
- Cualquier cosa que usted diga puede ser usada en su contra en una Corte de Ley o Tribunal Judicial.
- Usted tiene el derecho de hablar con un abogado y de que este presente durante la interrogacion
- Si usted no tiene los fondos para contratar a un abogado, la corte le asignara uno sin costo alguno para usted.

Entende usted sus derechos?

	derecha (izquierda)
(left)	
Give me your hand	Deme la mano
You in the car, we know you are there, sit up now	Ustedes en el carro, sabemos que estan ahi, sientense derechos ahora mismo
Front passenger	Pasajero delantero
Rear pasenger	Pasajero de atras

BASIC COMMANDS

English	Spanish
Come here	Venga aqui
come with me	venga conmigo
don't move	no se mueva
don't talk	no hable
drop the weapon	suelte el arma
follow me	sigame
give me your license	deme su licencia
get against the wall	pongase contra la pared
get out of the car	salga carro
go away	vayase
go over there	vaya alla
quickly/hurry up	rapido
raise your hands	levante las manos
repeat please	repita por favor
sit down	sientese
speak slower	hable mas despacio
stand up	parese
stay there	quedese ahi
stop	pare
tell me the truth	digame la verdad
you are under arrest	usted esta arrestado

Mayo	May
Julio	June
Agosto	August
Septiembre	September
Octubre	October
Noviembre	November
Diciembre	December

NUMBERS

1 - Uno	20 - Viente
2 - Dos	30 - Treinta
3 - Tres	40 - Cuarenta
4 - Cuatro	50 - Cincuenta
5 - Cinco	60 - Sesenta
6 - Seis	70 - Sententa
7 - Siete	80 - Ochenta
8 - Ocho	90 - Noventa
9 - Nueve	100 - Cien
10 - Diez	200 - Doscientos
11 - Once	300 - Trescientos
12 - Doce	400 - Cuatrocientos
13 - Trece	500 - Quinientos
14 - Catorce	600 - Seiscientos
15 - Quince	700 - Setecientos
16 - Diez y seis	800 - Ochocientos
17 - Diez y siete	900 - Novecientos
18 - Diez y ocho	1000 - Mil
19 - Diez y nueve	

NOTES

onal's country. In the
ation, assume this is the
ssport or other travel
ign national travels.

ational's country is not on the
notification list on page 36:

without delay, to notify the foreign
onal's consular officials of the arrest /
etention. Statement 1 on page 37; and,

✓ If the foreign national asks that consular
notification be given, notify the nearest consular
officials of the foreign national's country without
delay.

3 If the foreign national's country is on the list of
mandatory notification countries on page 36:
✓ Notify that country's nearest consular officials,
without delay, of the arrest / detention; and,
✓ Tell the foreign national that you are making this
notification. Statement 2 on page 37; and,

4 Keep a written record of the provision of
notification and actions taken.

5 [1]These steps should be followed for all foreign
nationals, regardless of their immigration status.

QUESTIONS

Assistant Legal Advisor for Consular Affairs
Department of State
202-647-4415 phone
202-736-7559 fax
Urgent after hours inquires
202 647 1512

ARREST & DETENTION OF FOREIGN NATIONALS

Mandatory Notification Countries

Antingua and Barbuba
Armenia
Azerbaijan
Bahamas, The
Barbados
Belarus
Belize
Brunei
Bulgaria
China[1]
Costa Rica
Cyprus
Czech Republic
Dominica
Fiji
Gambia, The
Georgia
Ghana
Grenada
Guyana
Hong Kong[2]
Hungary
Jamaica
Kazakhstan
Kiribati
Kuwait
Kyrgyzstan
Malaysia

Malta
Mongolia
Nigeria
Philipines
Poland (non-permanent citizens only)
Romania
Russia
Saint Kitts and Nevis
Saint Lucia
Saint Vincent and the Grenadines
Sychelles
Sierra Leone
Singapore
Slovakia
Tajikistan
Tanzania
Tonga
Tinidad and Tobago
Turkmenistan
Tuvalu
Ukraine
United Kingdom[3]
U.S.S.R[4]
Uzbekistan
Zambia
Zimbabwe

[1] Notification is not mandatory in the case of persons who carry "Republic of China" passports issued by . Such persons should be informed without delay that the nearest office of the Taipei Economic and Cultural Representative

...ficials of the
...rts in the same
...ese passports.
...by this agreement are
...rmuda, Montserrat, and
...sh passports.
...longer exists, some nationals of
...y still be traveling on its passports.
...on should be given to consular officers
...or such states, including those traveling on
...passports. The successor states are listed
...y above.

ARREST & DETENTION OF FOREIGN NATIONALS

Suggested Statements to Arrested or Detained Foreign Nationals

Statement 1:
When Consular Notification is at the Foreign National's Option

"As a non-U.S. citizen who is being arrested or detained, you are entitled to have us notify your country's consular representatives here in the . A consular official from your country may be able to help you obtain legal counsel, and may contact your family and visit you in detention, among other things. If you want us to notify your country's consular officials, you can request this notification now, or at any time in the future. After your consular officials are notified, they may call or visit you. Do you want us to notify your country's consular officials?"

When Consular Notification is Mandatory

"Because of your nationality, we are required to notify your country's consular representatives here in the that you have been arrested or detained. After your consular officials are notified, they may call or visit you. You are not required to accept their assistance, but they may be able to help you obtain legal counsel and may contact your family and visit you in detention, among other things. We will be notifying your country's consular officials as soon as possible.

Notes

Foreign

UNIVERSAL PRECAUTIONS

- ✓ Wear gloves for all patient contacts and for all contacts with body fluids
- ✓ Wash hands after patient contact
- ✓ Wear a mask for patients who are coughing or sneezing Place a mask on the patient too
- ✓ Wear eye shields or goggles when body fluids may splash
- ✓ Wear gowns when needed
- ✓ Wear utility gloves for cleaning equipment
- ✓ Don't recap, cut, or bend needles
- ✓ *Get vaccinated against Hepatitis A, B, and Meningitis A, C, W, Y

INFECTIOUS DISEASES

Disease...	Spread by...	Risk to you...
AIDS / HIV	IV / Sex / Blood products	↓ Immune function, Pneumonias, Cancer
ANTHRAX	Cutaneous: contact with skin lesions	Infection = 25% mortality, but much lower if treated
	Ingestion: eating contaminated meat	Infection = high mortality, unless treated with antibiotics
	Pulmonary: inhaled spores	Infection = 95% mortality, but much lower if treated
Hepatitis A*	Fecal-oral	Acute hepatitis
Hepatitis B*	IV / Sex / Birth / Blood	Acute & chronic hepatitis, Cirrhosis, Liver CA
Hepatitis C	Blood	Chronic hepatitis, Cirrhosis, Liver CA
Hepatitis D	IV / Sex / Birth	Chronic liver disease
Hepatitis E	Fecal-oral	↑ Mortality to pregnant women and fetus
Herpes	Skin contact	Skin lesions, shingles
Meningitis*	Nasal secretions	Low risk to rescuer
Tuberculosis	Sputum / cough / IV / Body fluids	Active tuberculosis, pulmonary infection

to report a blood borne exposure: _____

Report every exposure & seek immediate treatment!

[1]Inhalation Anthrax is not contagious from person-to-person contact

EMS

ALLERGIC REACTION

HX—Mild reaction (local swelling only); or Serious systemic reaction (hives, itching, pale skin, wheezing, upper airway obstruction, swelling of throat, low blood pressure, cardiac arrest)?
❖ If bee sting, remove stinger (scrape, don't squeeze).
  • For mild local reaction: wash area, apply cold pack.
  • For serious reaction: secure airway & ventilate. Use bee sting kit / EpiPen® as directed

Contra—Epinephrine may cause irregular pulse and/or chest pain

BURNS

HX—Was patient in enclosed space? How long? Was there an explosion? Toxic fumes? History of cardiac or lung disease? How long since burn? Other trauma?
Treatment
1 Stop the burning—extinguish smoldering clothing
2 Remove clothing if not adhered to skin
3 Remove jewelry
4 Protect airway & be prepared to assist ventilations
1st & 2nd Degree Burns
  • If ↓ 20%, apply wet dressing
Moderate to Severe Burns
  • Apply dry sterile dressing or burn sheet
  • Leave blisters intact
Chemical Burns
  • Brush off any dry chemical then flush with copious amounts of water
  • Lime: brush off excess, then flush
  • Phosphorus: alcohol or copious amounts of water
Electrical Burns
  • Apply dry sterile dressing to entry & exit wounds

HX—Onset of collapse, downtime? Was CPR started?
Surroundings: Is this drug-related or trauma-related?
Resuscitate unless obvious signs of morbidity, e.g.
rigor mortis. Request further information from family
members, physician, hospital.

Start CPR & attach AED as soon as it arrives.

head-tilt / chin lift

lower ½ of sternum

CPR	Ratio	Rate	Depth	Check Pulse
Adult: 1 Person	30:2	100	1-1/2"–2"	Carotid
Adult: 2 People	30:2	100	1-1/2"–2"	Carotid
Child: 1 Person	30:2	100	1/3–1/2 cx	Carotid
Child: 2 Person	15:2	100	1/3–1/2 cx	Carotid
Infant: 1 Person	15:2	100	1/3–1/2 cx	Brachial, Fem.

Adult, Child or Infant CPR

1 Determine unresponsiveness
2 Call for assistance (If child/infant, CPR x 1 min. first)
3 Position patient supine on hard, flat surface
4 Open airway: head-tilt / chin-lift (If trauma: jaw thrust)
5 Check breathing; if none: ventilate x 2
6 Check pulse; if none: chest compressions; 30:2;
   push hard & fast -- minimize interruptions in CPR
7 Attach AED to adult (& child ↑ 1 y.o.); follow voice
   prompts,
8 Recheck pulse after shocks and after 5 cycles of
   CPR (30 compressions: 2 breaths = 1 cycle)
9 Continue CPR if no pulse

DEFIBRILLATION - AED

1 Determine unresponsiveness
2 Check ABC's
   ✓ Airway
   ✓ Breathing
   ✓ Circulation

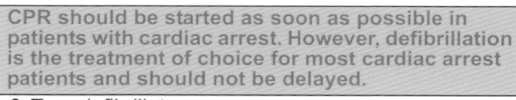

CPR should be started as soon as possible in patients with cardiac arrest. However, defibrillation is the treatment of choice for most cardiac arrest patients and should not be delayed.

3 Turn defibrillator on
4 Apply defibrillator pads
5 Analyze EKG rhythm
6 Deliver shocks as directed by AED
7 Continue CPR as directed by AED

NOTE: DO NOT...
- ...Use AED on patients under 1 year of age
- ...Use AED on wet surface
- ...Touch patient when analyzing rhythm
- ...Touch patient when delivering shock

CHEST PAIN

Treatment
1 Activate EMS
2 Place patient in position of comfort:
❖ lying down if dizzy
❖ sitting up if short of breath
Contra—DO NOT allow patient to exert himself / herself

CHEST TRAUMA

HX—Mechanism of injury — estimate forces involved; lung disease; medications; allergies; respiratory distress; pain; level of consciousness; skin color; is patient anxious? Symmetrical expansion of chest? Distended neck veins? Is patient coughing / spitting up blood?

Treatment
- Activate EMS
- Position of comfort
- Reassure patient
- Secure airway

Specific Treatments
- Open chest wound: cover with occlusive dressing and look for exit wound(s)
- Impaled objects: stabilize in place. Do not remove impaled object(s)

Life threatening chest injuries:
- Open chest wound(s)
- Tension pneumothorax (collapsed lung(s))
- Flail segment (2 or more ribs fractured in 2 or more places)

CHILDBIRTH

Most births are normal — reassure Mom & Dad

RX—Timing of contractions? intensity, does mother have urge to push or to move bowels? If so, birth is imminent. Prepare for immediate delivery. Has amniotic sac ruptured? Check for:

- ❑ **Vaginal bleeding or amniotic fluid**; note color of fluid
- ❑ **Crowning** (means imminent delivery)
- ❑ **Abnormal presentation**: foot, arm, breech, cord, shoulder

Normal: control delivery, suction mouth & nose, deliver, keep infant level with perineum, clamp & cut cord 8" – 10", **warm & dry infant**, stimulate infant by drying with towel, **make sure respirations are adequate**. Normal vital signs: Pulse ↑120, Resp ↑40. Baby should appear pink. If baby is blue, ventilate mouth-to-mouth. Give baby to mother to nurse at breast. If excessive postpartum bleeding, treat for shock, massage uterus to aid contraction, have mother nurse infant.

Breech: If head won't deliver, consider applying gentle pressure on mother's abdomen. If unsuccessful, insert two gloved fingers in vagina between baby's face and vaginal wall to create airway

Cord Presents: place mother in head down / legs elevated position, hold pressure on baby's head to relieve pressure on cord, check pulses in cord, keep cord moist with saline dressing

Foot / leg presentation: support presenting part, place mother in head down / legs elevated position

Cord around neck: unwrap cord from neck and deliver normally, keep face clear, suction mouth & nose, etc.

Infant not breathing: Stimulate with dry towel, rub back, flick soles of feet with finger. Suction mouth and nose. Ventilate (this will revive most infants). Begin chest compressions if no pulse. If child does not respond, reassess quality of ventilation efforts, failure to respond usually indicates lack of oxygen.

CHOKING

For Responsive Choking Adult or Child

1　If patient can not talk or has stridor, or cyanosis:
2　**Perform Heimlich Maneuver;** (may also use back slaps—use chest thrusts if pt is pregnant or obese) repeat until successful or pt. is unconscious:
3　**Activate EMS.** Begin CPR / Call for assistance
4　**Open airway;** head tilt-chin lift (look and remove object if visible):
5　**Ventilate with two breaths**—if unable:
6　**Reposition head;** attempt to ventilate—if unable:
7　**Perform chest compressions (30:2)**
8　**Repeat: inspect mouth → remove object → ventilate → chest compressions** until successful or EMS arrives.
9　**If pt. resumes breathing, place in the recovery position.**

For Unresponsive Choking Adult or Child

1　**Determine unresponsiveness**
2　**Activate EMS.** Begin CPR / Call for assistance
3　**Position patient supine** on hard, flat surface
4　**Open airway** — head-tilt / chin-lift; (look and remove object if visible):
5　**Attempt to ventilate** — if unable:
6　**Reposition head & chin, attempt to ventilate** — if unable:
7　**Perform chest compressions (30:2)**
8　**Attempt to ventilate**
9　**Repeat: inspect mouth → remove object → ventilate → chest compressions** until successful or EMS arrives.
10　**If pt. resumes breathing, place in the recovery position.**

EMS

For Choking Infant

1 **Tap infant, attempt to elicit response;** if infant can not make sounds, breathe, or is unresponsive;

2 **Invert infant on arm.** Support head by cupping face in hand. Perform 5 back slaps & 5 chest thrusts until object is expelled or pt becomes unconscious

3 Repeat until successful

4 **Activate EMS. If pt becomes unconscious, start CPR**

5 **Open airway & ventilate x 2;** if unable;

6 **Reposition head & chin, attempt to ventilate again;**

7 **Begin chest compressions 30:2.** and continue until successful or EMS arrives.

8 **If pt. resumes breathing, place in the recovery position.**

COMA / UNCONSCIOUS

HX—Ask General History questions
Rule out: trauma, infection, stroke, shock, hypoglycemia, drugs, alcohol, toxic exposure, seizures, tumor, electrolyte imbalance, fever, head injury. Time of onset? Were there any preceding symptoms or headache?
Past Hx: High blood pressure, diabetes? Medications? Medic Alert™ tag? Check the scene for pill bottles or syringes and bring with patient.
Ensure your safety first, then safety of victim & others!
Treatment:
• Secure airway
• Protect cervical-spine
• Monitor vital signs

NOTE:
• Protect airway
• If multiple patients — suspect toxins

DROWNING & NEAR DROWNING

HX—How long was patient in the water? Salt or fresh water? Cold water (↓ 40 F)?

Treatment
- **Activate EMS**
- Secure airway
- Assist ventilations if needed
- CPR if needed
- Warm pt. if cold

NOTE:
- Diving accident — immobilize spine
- Unconscious — immobilize spine
- Prepare for vomiting

FRACTURES & DISLOCATIONS

HX—Mechanism of injury. Localized pain, point tenderness, guarding, swelling, deformity, angulation, discoloration, limited range of motion? Lacerations, exposed bone fragments?

Treatment
- **Activate EMS**
- ABC's
- Control bleeding
- Immobilize spine as indicated by pain or mechanism
- Check for additional injuries
- Treat for shock as indicated
- Apply dressings to open wounds
- Splint fractures
- Elevate simple extremity fractures
- Apply cold pack as needed

NOTE:
- Two or more fractures of femur / humerus = significant trauma
- Extremity fractures are lower priority when treating the multisystem trauma patient

EMS

HEAD INJURY

HX—Mechanism of injury, estimate forces involved. Any changes in level of consciousness? Amnesia? Was seatbelt, helmet worn? Respiratory rate, pattern, quality? Chest or trunk injuries? Blood or clear fluid from ears or nose? Scalp, skull depression, associated facial trauma?

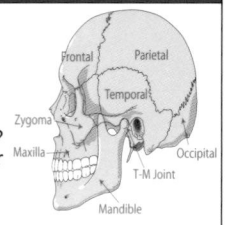

Treatment
- **Activate EMS**
- Secure airway while providing c-spine immobilization
- Control bleeding with direct pressure
- Do not control bleeding from ears / nose
- Assist ventilations as needed

NOTE:
- Always suspect c-spine injury in the head injury patient

HEAT STROKE / HYPERTHERMIA

HX—Onset? Exercise- or drug- (cocaine) induced? Temperature? Skin: warm / dry (heat stroke = no sweating)
Treatment
- Remove from hot environment
- **Activate EMS**
- Secure airway
- Undress (ensure privacy) and begin cooling
- Consider cold packs to groin and armpits
- Evaporation & convection measures work best

NOTE:
- Rapid cooling is the most important treatment

HYPOTHERMIA

HX—Mental status. Is patient cold? Shivering?
Evidence of local injury?

Treatment
- **Activate EMS**
- Secure airway
- Remove from cold environment
- Cut off wet clothing (handle patient gently)
- Wrap in warm blankets
- If cardiac arrest — start CPR

NOTE:
- Handle gently — jostling can cause cardiac arrest
- If not shivering — do not let patient walk
- Stimulating the airway can cause cardiac arrest
- "If ONLY hypothermic, no patient is dead until they are warm and dead"

OC AFTER-CARE

HX—Once subject has been controlled with OC and properly restrained, begin the following after-care:

Treatment
- Move subject to fresh air
- Activate EMS for evaluation
- If subject wears contact lenses, remove when safe
- Reassure subject that OC effects are temporary
- Flush subject's face with water & apply wet towel
- Notify corrections personnel that subject has been sprayed with OC

NOTE:
- Avoid touching your own eyes, nose, mouth, until your hands are thoroughly washed
- DO NOT leave the subject unattended

WARNING: If subject has difficulty breathing, increased body temperature, flaccid muscle tone, and / or increased ability to sustain a fight, subject is at HIGH RISK for Sudden In-Custody Death. Call EMS.

POISONING / OVERDOSE

HX—Type, time, quantity of ingestion? Bring pill bottle to Emergency Department. Is patient suicidal? Is this child neglect?

Treatment — External Contamination
- **Activate EMS**
- Remove contaminated clothing from patient
- Flush contaminated skin & eyes with copious amounts of water

NOTE: Protect yourself from contamination. If multiple patients, beware of HazMat.

Treatment — Internal Ingestion
- **Activate EMS**
- Contact Poison Control
- ABC's

WARNING: Inhalation poisoning is particularly dangerous to rescuers. Recognize an environment with continuing contamination and extricate rapidly using properly trained and equipped personnel

SEIZURES

HX—Onset, length of seizure, type of seizure, previous Hx? Seizure medications? Recent head trauma, diabetes, drugs, alcohol, pregnancy, stroke, heart condition? What was the patient doing before seizure? Drug-induced (antidepressant, cocaine)? Medic Alert? Head or oral trauma?

Treatment
- **Activate EMS**
- Keep airway open
- Most seizures are benign and last only 1 – 2 minutes

NOTE:
- Restrain patient only to prevent injury
- Protect the patient's head
- Do not force anything into the patient's mouth

SHOCK

HX—Mental status: confusion, restlessness?
Increased heart rate, decreased blood pressure?
Skin: pale, sweaty, cool.

Treatment
- **Activate EMS**
- Stop hemorrhage if any
- Direct pressure to wound
- Consider use of pressure points
- Lay patient down with feet up
- Minimize heat loss

SPINAL INJURY

HX—Suspect cervical-spine injury with head or neck
trauma, and with multi-system trauma. Is there
altered mental status? Is there paralysis, weakness,
numbness, tingling in extremities?

Treatment
- Keep airway open
- Splint neck with cervical collar
- Immobilize entire spine
- Move patient as unit and only move as necessary

NOTE:
- If patient vomits, move the patient as a unit on
  his/her side to clear vomitus
- Consider internal bleeding

STROKE

HX—Past Hx: high blood pressure, diabetes, medic
alert tag? Level of consciousness? Slurred speech,
difficulty understanding? Weakness on one side?

Treatment
- Keep airway open
- Be prepared to assist ventilations

96

EMS

K-9 MEDICAL EMERGENCIES

ENSURE OFFICER SAFETY!

1 Purpose of K-9 EMS
- ✓ Relieve suffering
- ✓ Stabilize the dog's vital signs until professional help is obtained

2 Handling An Injured Dog
- ✓ Approach the dog slowly, speaking in a reassuring tone of voice
- ✓ Move toward dog without touching it
- ✓ Stoop and observe its eyes and facial expression
- ✓ If dog is growling do not attempt to pet it
  - Place leash around dog's neck and tie to fixed object
  - Pull dog against object
  - Secure leash so that dog cannot move it's head
- ✓ Place muzzle on dog
- ✓ Emergency muzzle can be made from cloth, neck tie, etc.
  - Loop around jaws and tie single knot under chin
  - Bring ends up and behind ears and tie in bow
- ✓ Once secured with muzzle, begin evaluation

3 A = Airway
- ✓ Determine if dog is breathing
  - Decreased level of consciousness or inadequate respirations, begin rescue breathing
- ✓ If unconscious and not breathing - suspect airway obstruction
  - Extend the neck, pull the tongue forward, sweep the mouth with your finger
  - Give 5 abdominal thrusts
  - Repeat finger sweep and ventilate dog

4 B = Breathing
- ✓ Artificial Respiration
  - Place dog on a firm flat surface
  - Open the mouth and clear airway debris / fluids
  - Grasp the tongue and pull it forward and close the mouth
  - Seal the lips with your hand

- Blow in steadily for 3 seconds
- Release and allow air to come out
- Ventilate at a rate of 20 breaths / minute
- Continue until dog breathes on its own, or for as long as a heartbeat can be felt

5 C = Circulation
✓ Check for heartbeat
  - Place two fingers firmly on the dog's chest about 2" behind its elbow in the center of its chest
✓ Cardiac Massage
  - When no heartbeat is felt or heard
  - Place dog on a flat surface
  - Place heel of your hand on the ribcage just behind the elbow, which is the area over the heart
  - Perform simultaneous chest compressions with ventilations every 2 to 3 compressions
  - Chest compressions should continue at a rate of 80 – 120 per minute
  - Continue chest compressions until the dog has a heartbeat or until no pulse can be detected for 5 minutes

6 Shock
✓ Signs of Shock: shivering, listlessness, weakness, cold feet, pale skin, pale gums, weak pulse
✓ If no breathing or pulse is found, proceed with CPR
✓ Lift upper lip to examine gums
✓ Determine heart rate (↓ 150 / min = shock)
✓ Elevate hindquarters to increase blood flow to brain
✓ Control bleeding with direct pressure
✓ Cover dog with warm blanket
✓ Give oxygen if available
✓ Immediately transport to veterinarian

7 Wound Care
✓ Objectives: Stop Bleeding & Prevent Shock
  - Arterial bleeding — bright red spurting blood
  - Venous bleeding — oozing dark red blood

- ✓ Pressure dressing: Take several pieces of clean or sterile gauze and place them directly over the wound & apply firm, even pressure
- ✓ After bleeding is controlled, apply bandage

8 Transportation
- ✓ Do not move dog more than necessary
- ✓ Notify department veterinarian
- ✓ Moderate injuries: Lift dog by placing one arm around chest and other around back legs
- ✓ Suspected spinal injury: place dog on backboard
  - Ensure backboard fits in transport vehicle
  - Place board next to dog
  - Put the straps underneath the board
  - Gently lift or slide dog onto board
  - Secure dog to board with straps
  - Cover dog with warm blanket

Department Veterinarian
Name:

_____

Address:

_____

Phone:

_____

Mental Status Evaluation (MSE)

When dealing with an unknown person, you may have to quickly assess their mental and cognitive abilities. This checklist provides some common symptoms of mental impairment. **Multiple symptoms mean that the patient should be further evaluated by a mental health worker as soon as possible.**

Be aware that it may be difficult to ascertain if a person is mentally challenged, mentally ill, or using mind or mood-altering drugs.

1 Speak calmly, clearly, and use simple words.
2 Do not argue with the patient and do not attempt to convince or coerce them to follow requests. **Tell them what to do, calmly and repeatedly.**
   Remember, they are not able to think clearly, so you will not be able to use rational thought with them.

EXAMPLE: If the patient tells you he is scared, don't tell them they shouldn't be scared. Instead, say "I understand you are scared, tell me why."

3 If safe, gently lead the person with a very light touch to the position or place where you want them to be. **Do not use force** unless absolutely necessary.

Appearance

☐ Lack of hygiene?

☐ Hostile or frightened attitude?
☐ Unusual/foul odors?

☐ Non-age appropriate clothes?
☐ Non-gender appropriate clothes?
☐ Signs of mutilation/ suicide attempts?

Behavior

☐ Odd gestures?
☐ Picking at self?

☐ Odd posturing?
☐ Touching caregiver?

Movement

- ☐ Agitated?
- ☐ Slow?
- ☐ Uncoordinated?
- ☐ Tics or twitches?
- ☐ Unusual gait?
- ☐ Rocking or hand flapping?

Speech

- ☐ Monotonous tone?
- ☐ Slurred speech?
- ☐ Slow reaction?
- ☐ Rapid speech?
- ☐ Repeating your words?
- ☐ Jumbled or out of order?

Mood

- ☐ Obviously depressed?
- ☐ Terrified for no reason?
- ☐ Overly angry?
- ☐ Elated for no reason?
- ☐ Overly anxious?
- ☐ Claims of guilt and remorse?

Thoughts

- ☐ Rapid 'Flight of ideas'?
- ☐ Loose associations?
- ☐ Preoccupations?
- ☐ Suicidal?
- ☐ Slow associations?
- ☐ Delusions?
- ☐ Hallucinations?
- ☐ Homicidal?

Cognition

- ☐ Can't remember name?
- ☐ Don't know month/ year?
- ☐ Short-term memory impairment
- ☐ Do not know location?
- ☐ Doesn't get situation?
- ☐ Long-term memory impairment?

HAZARDOUS MATERIALS

ENSURE OFFICER SAFETY—CONSIDER BEST APPROACH WHEN DISPATCHED

1 If suspected HazMat incident, call for HazMat Team:
   - ✓ Uphill, upwind, upstream from incident
   - ✓ Stage at least 500 ft. away from accident (distance should be determined by Department protocols, type of incident, etc.)

2 Establish Incident Command Structure Immediately

3 Establish Safety Perimeter
   - ✓ ISOLATE area & DENY entry
   - ✓ Stop traffic, evacuate if needed

4 You May Have to Delay Rescue to Identify Hazards
   - ✓ Attempt to identify product, use binoculars, look for placards

5 Identify Safe Areas
   - ✓ HOT, WARM, and COLD zones (see page 103)
   - ✓ Protective clothing & respiratory protection needed for rescue
   - ✓ Decon level needed for material (specific or field decon)
   - ✓ Evacuation distances if appropriate
   - ✓ Protect people, environment (Dam, Dike, Divert)

6 Consider mapping the area & drawing a rough diagram showing:
   - ✓ Routes of access / egress
   - ✓ Location of HazMat spill
   - ✓ Topography and drainage
   - ✓ Wind direction
   - ✓ Exposures
   - ✓ Evacuation problems & distances

WARNING: If product is unknown, use DOT Guide 111 for general safety precautions until product can be identified.

HazMat

ROAD TANKERS

FLAMMABLE LIQUID TANKER

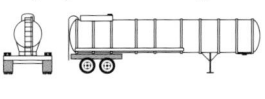

- Oval shape, dome cover on top
- Flammable, combustible, other liquid (not compressed gas)
- Usually load and off-load through bottom valves
- Stainless or aluminum
- Minimal BLEVE potential, rapid burn-through

CORROSIVE LIQUID TANKER

- Round in diameter, with reinforcing rings
- Slightly rounded, blunt ends
- Smaller in diameter than pressurized gas tanker
- Stainless or aluminum construction
- Loads and unloads through valves at rear
- May contain poisons, oxidizers, haz. waste, corrosives
- Moderate to high BLEVE potential when impinged by fire

CRYOGENIC LIQUID TANKER

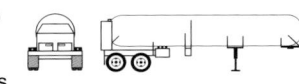

- Very large, round diameter, blunt ends
- Inner and outer tank, like thermos
- Loading and unloading through "box" at rear
- May contain corrosives, flammable gas, poisons, oxidizer
- Will not have a high pressure gas (usually ↓ 25 psi)

COMPRESSED GAS

- Perfectly round diameter, steel construction
- Evenly rounded ends
- Loads, unloads through bottom valves
- May have flammable, nonflammable, oxidizer gas
- Stay away / stage away from ends of tank
- High BLEVE potential when impinged by fire

RAIL TANKERS

PRESSURIZED RAIL CARS

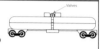

- Always loaded and unloaded from the top
- PSI may range from 100 PSI to 600 PSI
- Valves and gauges are often in a dome at the top
- Valves and gauges are often in a dome at the top
- Stay away from tank ends
- Position in a defensive manner

GENERAL SERVICE (NON-PRESSURIZED) CARS

- Unloaded from valves at bottom or vapor recovery
- Can be loaded from dome, bottom valves or vapor recovery connection

ID Markings on All Rail Cars (Example: DOT III A 60 AL W I)	
DOT	Authorizing agency
III	Class Type
A	Protection systems (or Separation Letter)
60	Tank test pressure (psi)
AL	Tank material if other than steel
W	Construction — Welded
I	Valve and fitting types

HAZARD CONTROL ZONES

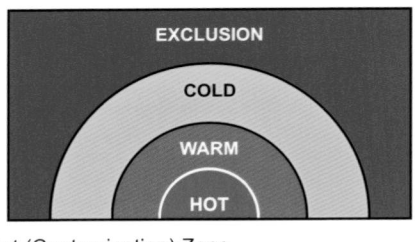

1 Hot (Contamination) Zone
- ✓ Contamination or danger of explosion is actually present
- ✓ Personnel must wear appropriate gear
- ✓ Limit number of rescuers to those absolutely necessary

2 Warm (Control) Zone
- ✓ Area surrounding the contamination zone
- ✓ Vital to preventing spread of contamination
- ✓ Personnel must wear appropriate protective gear
- ✓ Life-saving emergency care and decontamination are performed

3 Cold (Safe) Zone
- ✓ Normal triage, stabilization and treatment performed
- ✓ Rescuers must shed contaminated gear before entering the cold zone
- ✓ I/C and Command Post are normally located within the Cold Zone

4 Exclusion Zone — Public Area
- ✓ Zone for the public and non-operational personnel (e.g. media, public officials)

SHIPPING PLACARD USAGES

NFPA 704 HazMat* Classification

HEALTH HAZARD
4 - Deadly
3 - Extreme danger
2 - Hazardous
1 - Slightly Hazardous
0 - Normal Material

FIRE HAZARD
Flash Points
4 - Below 73 F
3 - Below 100 F
2 - Below 200 F
1 - Above 200 F
0 - Will not burn

SPECIFIC HAZARD
Oxidixer — OXY
Acid — ACID
Alkali — ALK
Corrosive — COR
Simple Asphyxiant — SA
Use NO WATER — ₩
Radiation Hazard — ☢

REACTIVITY
4 - May detonante
3 - Shock / heat may detonate
2 - Violent chemical change
1 - Unstable if heated
0 - Stable

* Not intended to identify non-emergency heath hazards

Numbered Placard
DOT ID Number (fuel) and
Class (flammable liquid)

Placard and Orange Panel
Used to indicate hazard & specific
compound (here, acetone)

106

HazMat

HAZMAT SHIPPING PLACARDS

DANGEROUS
Guide 111

COMBUSTIBLE
3
Guide 127

SPONTANEOUSLY
COMBUSTIBLE
4
Guide 136

FUEL OIL
3
Guide 128

FLAMMABLE
SOLID
4
Guide 134

FLAMMABLE
GAS
2
Guide 118

DANGEROUS WHEN WET
4
Guide 139

OXIDIZER
5.1
Guide 143

W
FLAMMABLE
SOLID
4
Guide 139

EXPLOSIVES
A
1
Guide 112

RADIOACTIVE
7
Guide 163

1.4
EXPLOSIVE
*
1
Guide 114

material
- ✓ Discontinue use of all radios, MDTs and cell phones in accordance with local protocol
- ✓ Remove all citizens and ambulatory victims from affected area
- ✓ Determine on-scene conditions and resource requirements:
  - Explosion / Fire
  - Structural collapse / unstable buildings
  - Search / Rescue (non-ambulatory / trapped victims)
  - Exposures
  - Utilities
  - Make local, state and federal notifications
  - Complete Hazard and Risk Assessment

Terror

EXPLOSIVES EVACUATION TABLE

ATFE	DESCRIPTION	MAXIMUM EXPLOSIVES CAPACITY	LETHAL AIR BLAST RANGE	MINIMUM EVACUATION DISTANCE	FALLING GLASS HAZARD
	Briefcase	33 lbs / 15 kg	Variable*	1123 ft / 342 m	Variable*
	Compact Sedan or Small Package	500 lbs / 227 kg (in trunk)	100 ft / 30 m	1500 ft / 457 m	1250 ft / 381 m
	Full Size Sedan	1000 lbs / 455 kg (in trunk)	125 ft / 38 m	1750 ft / 534 m	1750 ft / 534 m
	Passenger Van or Cargo Van	4000 lbs / 1818 kg	200 ft / 61 m	2750 ft / 838 m	2750 ft / 838 m
	Small Box Van (14-foot box)	10000 lbs / 4545 kg	300 ft / 91 m	3750 ft / 1143 m	3750 ft / 1143 m
	Box Van or Water / Fuel Truck	30000 lbs / 13636 kg	450 ft / 137 m	6500 ft / 1982 m	6500 ft / 1982 m
	Semi-Trailer	60000 lbs / 27273 kg	600 ft / 183 m	7000 ft / 2134 m	7000 ft / 2134 m

*Smaller package bombings are too complex to accurately predict distance for all situations.

Source: Bureau of Alcohol, Tobacco, Firearms and Explosives document ATF 1540

HazMat

CLANDESTINE DRUG LABS

ENSURE OFFICER SAFETY

If you encounter a Clan Lab or suspected Clan Lab — GET OUT!

Notify if you or another individual is injured by chemicals in a clandestine lab

1 Safety Guidelines
- ✓ DO NOT touch anything in the lab
- ✓ DO NOT turn on OR on any electrical power or light switches
- ✓ DO NOT eat or drink in or around a lab
- ✓ DO NOT open or move containers containing chemicals or suspected chemicals
- ✓ DO NOT smoke anywhere near a lab
- ✓ DO NOT sniff containers

2 Decontamination
- ✓ DO decontaminate yourself, clothing, and gear
- ✓ DO wash your hands and face very well

3 Clan Lab Indicators
- ✓ Large amount of cold tablet containers that contain
- ✓ Ephedrine or Pseudoephedrine
- ✓ Jars w/clear liquid & white colored solid on top
- ✓ Jars containing Red Phosphorus or a fine dark red or purple powder
- ✓ Coffee filters containing white pasty substance, dark red sludge, or small amount of shiny white crystals
- ✓ Sulfuric Acid or Hydrochloric Acid
- ✓ Bottles / jars w/rubber tubing attached
- ✓ Glass cookware / frying pans w/powdery residue
- ✓ Large amounts of Coleman fuel, paint thinner, acetone, starting fluid, Red Devil lye, Muriatic Acid, drain cleaners containing Sulfuric Acid

stored in oil or Kerosene
- ✓ Propane tanks with fittings that have turned blue
- ✓ Occupants of residence going outside to smoke
- ✓ Strong smell of urine, ether, ammonia, or acetone

4 Booby-Traps in Clan Labs
- ✓ Light switches wired to flammable liquid
- ✓ Explosive light bulbs
- ✓ Refrigerator doors wired to detonate when opened
- ✓ Video tape cassettes altered to detonate when played in VCR
- ✓ Monofilament trip lines connect to chemical / explosive
- ✓ Attack dogs & poisonous / dangerous snakes
- ✓ Pipe bombs / weapons / other obvious devices

5 Minimizing the Effects of a Booby-Trap
- ✓ Visually check everything before you touch it
- ✓ Inspect furniture before use
- ✓ Use caution with all electrical appliances
- ✓ DO NOT use light switches or interior lights
- ✓ DO NOT open refrigerator or other electrically-charged appliances
- ✓ DO NOT open or touch containers w/o thorough exterior inspection
- ✓ Use your eyes, nose, and ears when inside a booby- trapped area
- ✓ Stay alert and be ready for anything

HazMat

6 Call The Clan Lab Unit nearest you at the number below:

Atlanta 404-331-4401
Boston 617-557-2100
Caribbean 787-253-4200
Chicago 312-353-7875
Dallas 214-640-0801
Denver 303-705-7300
Detroit 313-234-4000
El Paso 915-534-6400
Houston 713-693-3000
Los Angeles 213-894-2650
Miami 305-590-4870

Newark 973-273-5000
New Orleans 504-840-1100
New York 212-337-3900
Philadelphia 215-597-9530
Phoenix 602-664-5600
San Diego 619-616-4100
San Francisco 415-436-7900
Seattle 206-553-5443
St. Louis 314-538-4600
Washington 202-305-8500

WARNING: Clan Labs are extremely dangerous. Many of the chemicals are very corrosive or flammable. The vapors that are released from the chemical reactions attack mucous membranes, skin, eyes, and the respiratory tract. Some chemicals will react with water and may cause a fire or explosion.

PRODUCTS COMMONLY FOUND IN CLANDESTINE DRUG LABS

Commercial Product	Chemicals	Hazards	Uses
Aluminum foil	Aluminum	Non-hazardous	Forms metal complex
Camera batteries	Lithium	Water reactive	Forms metal complex
Charcoal lighter fluid	Petroleum distillates	Flammable	Oil extraction
Denatured alcohol	Mixture of alcohol	Flammable	Tablet extraction
Epsom salts	Magnesium sulfate	Non-hazardous	Absorbs water
Gasoline	Petroleum distillates	Flammable	Oil extraction
Heet	Methyl alcohol	Flammable	Tablet extraction
Iodine crystals/ 7% tincture of iodine	Iodine	Irritant	Forms complex with ephedrine/pseudoeph.
Kerosene	Petroleum distillates	Flammable	Oil extraction
Lacquer thinner	Petroleum distillates	Flammable	Oil extraction
Mineral spirits	Petroleum distillates	Flammable	Oil extraction
Red Devil lye	Sodium hydroxide	Corrosive base	Adjusts pH
Drain Cleaner/Battery Acid	Sulfuric acid	Corrosive acid	Reacts with salt
Starting fluid	Ethyl ether	Flammable	Oil extraction
Striker plate	Phosphorus		Red phosphorus
Table salt	Sodium chloride	Non-hazardous	Reacts with sulfuric acid to form hydrochloric acid gas
OTC Cold meds	Ephedrine/Pseudoeph	Non-hazardous	Required for synthesis

112

Notes

TERRORIST ACTION

- Evaluate the scene for safety hazards
- Establish safety/hazard zones
- Communicate hazards to other responders
- Approach in a manner to reduce risk to officers

WARNING: Beware of incendiary or explosive devices! Do not touch any suspected incendiary or explosive device. Evacuate the area, and request the services of personnel trained in the removal of such items.

1 Initial Response
- ✓ Determine if scene is secured
- ✓ Use aerial / street maps to determine best location for:
  - Command Post: neutral ground, outside perimeter
  - Media
  - Staging
  - Ambulance access and egress
  - "Safe Zones" for victims and rescue personnel
  - Family staging area
- ✓ Determine: HOT - WARM - COLD zones (see page 103)
- ✓ Establish Unified Command and Law Enforcement ICS Branch

2 Access & Egress
- ✓ Secure access to area
- ✓ DO NOT block roads
- ✓ DO NOT park vehicle in positions that block roads

Terror

3 Prepare for Large Scale Operation
- ✓ Order and stage resources for:
  - Fire
  - EMS
  - HazMat Operations
  - Bomb Squad
  - Buses for transportation
  - Additional law enforcement resources

4 Operations
- ✓ Develop a plan of action
- ✓ Establish & communicate objectives to all

POTENTIAL AREAS OF VULNERABILITY

ENSURE OFFICER SAFETY

Areas at risk may be determined by several points: population, accessibility, economic impact, and symbolic value. This guide provides a general list of potential areas of vulnerability in your jurisdiction.

1 Traffic
- ✓ Roads / tunnels / bridges carrying large volumes of traffic
- ✓ Points of congestion that could impede response or place citizens in a vulnerable area

2 Trucking & Transport Activity
- ✓ Location of HazMat cargo loading / unloading facilities
- ✓ Vulnerable areas such as weigh stations & rest areas this cargo may transit

3 Waterways
- ✓ Pipelines & process / treatment facilities
- ✓ Berths & ports for cruise ships, roll-on / roll-off cargo vessels, and container ships
- ✓ International flagged vessels that conduct business in the area

- Air traffic control towers, runways, passenger terminals, and parking areas
5 **Trains / Subways**
  - ✓ Rails & lines, interchanges, terminals, tunnels, and cargo/passenger terminals
  - ✓ HazMat that may be transported via rail
6 **Government Facilities**
  - Federal / State / Local government offices
  - Post office, law enforcement stations, fire / rescue, town / city hall, and local mayor / governor's residences
7 **Recreation / Other Facilities**
  - ✓ Sports arenas, theaters, malls, & special interest group facilities
  - ✓ Financial institutions, military installations, HazMat facilities, utilities, dams, and nuclear facilities

ACTIVE SHOOTER RESPONSE

ENSURE OFFICER SAFETY

1 **Determine if Situation Requires Immediate Entry:**
  - ✓ Is violence actually taking place?
  - ✓ Is it occurring now?
  - ✓ If yes — make immediate entry.
  - ✓ Follow your agency "Active Shooter Protocol."

OBJECTIVE: LOCATE and STOP the active shooter. The only way to minimize casualties is to stop shooter. Preoccupation with evacuation, treatment and searching allows shooter to increase body count. REMAIN FOCUSED: Encounter shooter quickly, force surrender decision and get to the injured.

2 **Communications:**
  - ✓ Notify Dispatch Center of entry
  - ✓ Advise Dispatch Center of entry location(s)

3 **Four Officer Response**
(modified diamond
formation):

✓ Point officer: long cover
and all threats to front.
✓ Right guard: next
unsecured area to right.
Only concern is moving
formation safely past next doorway.
✓ Left guard: next unsecured area to left. Only
concern is moving formation safely past next
doorway.
✓ Rear guard: protection of formation from threats to
rear.

NOTE: Right / Left guards must fight urge to cover
long on hallway and maintain focus on doorways.
Point / Rear officers must maintain focus on area
of responsibility or risk safety / success of mis-
sion.

BIOLOGICAL AGENTS

ENSURE OFFICER SAFETY

1 **Bioattack Clues:**
✓ Large numbers of ill persons with a similar
disease or syndrome and / or many ill persons
who seek treatment at about the same time.
✓ An increase in unexplained disease and / or
death.
✓ Unusual illness in a population (e.g. renal disease
in a large population may suggest exposure to a
toxic agent such as mercury).
✓ Higher morbidity and mortality in association with
a common disease or syndrome or failure of such
patients to respond to usual therapy.

agent (e.g. smallpox, viral hemorrhagic fever, pulmonary anthrax).
- ✓ Several unusual or unexplained diseases coexisting in the same patient without any other explanation.
- ✓ Disease with unusual geographic / seasonal distribution (e.g. tularemia in a non-endemic area, influenza in the summer).
- ✓ Unusual / atypical illness for a given population / age group.
- ✓ Unusual disease presentation.
- ✓ Atypical disease transmission through aerosols, food, water; which suggest deliberate sabotage.

2 Biological Agents:
- ✓ Inhalation is primary route of entry
- ✓ Dermal is secondary route of entry
- ✓ SCBA and structural fire fighting gear provides adequate protection for first responders (Tyvek® is sufficient)

NOTE: Biological agents generally produce delayed symptoms.

3 Response Recommendations:
- ✓ Position uphill, upwind and away from building exhaust systems
- ✓ Isolate / secure the area (NAERG [orange book] #158 recommends initial isolation distance of 80 feet).
- ✓ Do not allow unprotected individuals to enter area
- ✓ Be alert for small explosive devices designed to disseminate the agent
- ✓ Gather information:
  - Type and form of agent (liquid, powder, aerosol)
  - Method of delivery
  - Location in structure

Terror

4 **Wet / Dry Agent from Point Source:**
   - ✓ Personnel entering area must wear full PPE including SCBA
   - ✓ Avoid contact with puddles, wet surfaces, etc.
   - ✓ Isolate area of building
   - ✓ Keep all potentially exposed individuals in close proximity, but out of the high-hazard area
   - ✓ Shut down HVAC system that services the area
   - ✓ If victims have visible agent on them:
     - exposed skin with soap and water
     - If highly contaminated (i.e., splashed) and the facility is equipped with showers, the victim(s) may shower and change clothes as a precaution
     - HazMat team may be able to conduct a bio assay field test

5 **Threat of Dry Agent Placed into HVAC or Package with No Physical Evidence:**
   - ✓ Isolate the building
     - Keep all potentially exposed victims in the building
     - Shut down all HVAC systems for the building
   - ✓ Collect information regarding the threat, target or any previous activity to gauge the credibility of the threat
     - Initiate a search of the building
     - Personnel entering area must wear full PPE, including SCBA
     - Avoid contact with puddles, wet surfaces, etc.
     - Investigate all HVAC intakes, returns, etc., for evidence of agent or dispersal equipment
     - If any evidence of an agent is found in / near the HVAC system, remove occupants from the building and isolate them in a secure and comfortable location
     - If a suspicious package is found, handle as a point source event

(visible fogger, sprayer or aerosolizing device)
- ✓ Personnel entering must wear full PPE and SCBA
- ✓ Avoid contact with puddles, wet surfaces, etc.
- ✓ Remove occupants from building / area and isolate
- ✓ Shut down HVAC system(s)
- ✓ HazMat team may be able to conduct bioassay field test (limited number of agents)

7 Treatment of exposed persons
- ✓ Decontaminate or shower, according to local protocols
- ✓ Place all possibly contaminated clothing / items in evidence collection bags
- ✓ Have provide any needed medical care

NUCLEAR / RADIOLOGICAL AGENTS

ENSURE RESPONDER SAFETY

1 General Information:
- ✓ Radiological agents may produce delayed reactions
- ✓ Exposed / contaminated victims may not exhibit obvious injuries
- ✓ Unlike exposure to chemical agents, exposure to radiological agents does NOT require immediate removal of victim's clothing or gross decon in the street
- ✓ Inhalation is the primary route of entry for particulate radiation
- ✓ In most cases, HEPA masks, goggles and structural fire fighting clothing provide adequate protection for first responders
- ✓ Gamma sources require minimizing exposure time and maintaining distance as the only protection

2 Response Recommendations:

- ✓ Position upwind of any suspected event
- ✓ Isolate / secure the area
- ✓ Be alert for small explosive devices designed to disseminate radioactive agent(s)
- ✓ Use time, distance and shielding as protective measures
- ✓ Use full PPE including SCBA
- ✓ Avoid contact with agent. Stay out of any visible smoke or fumes
- ✓ Measure background radiation levels outside of suspected area
  - Monitor radiation levels
  - Remove victims from high-hazard area to a safe holding area
  - Triage, treat and decontaminate trauma victims as appropriate
- ✓ Detain or isolate uninjured persons or equipment
- ✓ Delay decontamination for such persons / equipment until instructed by radiation authorities
- ✓ Use radiation detection devices, if possible, to determine if patients are contaminated with radiological material

INCENDIARY AGENTS

ENSURE OFFICER SAFETY

1 General Information

- ✓ Fire may present intense conditions:
  - Rapid spread
  - High heat
  - Multiple fires
  - Chemical accelerant
- ✓ Terrorists may sabotage fire protection devices
- ✓ Be alert for booby traps
- ✓ Be aware of the possibility of multiple devices

Incident Management

This section contains two parts:
- **Major Incident Management and Guidelines**— Contains updated information from NIMS and is for use during a major event which requires extensive coordination with other first responders such as EMS and Fire.
- **Routine Incident Management and Guidelines**—Contains information more routinely encountered and generally does not require major coordination with other first responders.

Major Incident Management & Guidelines

Ensure responder safety with personal protective measures and shielding as necessary.

1 Establish Command
2 Select and Set Up Command Post:
   ✓ Neutral ground, outside inner perimeter or cold zone, but within security perimeter
   ✓ Assess command post security
3 Ensure Scene Security:
   ✓ Isolate area / deny entry
4 Assess Staging:
   ✓ Provide, identify, designate safe staging location(s) for incoming units
5 Assess Emergency Egress Routes:
   ✓ Position apparatus to facilitate rapid evacuation
   ✓ If you must use emergency egress reassemble at designated rally point(s)
6 Designate Incident Safety Officer (see page 34):
   ✓ Ensure personal accountability system is in place

7 **Consider Liaison or Public Information Officer Position(s)**

8 **Assess Decontamination Requirements:**
   - ✓ Gross decontamination
   - ✓ Mass decontamination

9 **Consider Need For Additional / Specialized Resources:**
   - ✓ Fire / EMS / HazMat
   - ✓ Law Enforcement / Explosive Ordinance Disposal (EOD)
   - ✓ Public Works / Public Health / Environmental

10 **Consider event as a Potential Crime Scene:**
   - ✓ Consider everything at site as potential evidence
   - ✓ Ensure coordination with law enforcement

11 **Make Appropriate Notifications:**
   - ✓ Update situation report
   - ✓ Hospitals / Utilities / Law Enforcement as appropriate

12 **Prepare for Transition to Unified Command**

13 **Ensure Coordination for Communications:**
   - ✓ Identify Needs

14 **Order Resources**

Examples When ICS Should Be Used

1 **Incidents (unplanned occurrences):**
   - ✓ Major Traffic Collision
   - ✓ Hostage Situation
   - ✓ Bomb Incident
   - ✓ Air Crash
   - ✓ Hazardous Materials Spill
   - ✓ Officer-Involved Shooting
   - ✓ Civil Disorder / Riot
   - ✓ Fires and Explosions
   - ✓ Landslide

    ✓ Large Sporting / Concert Event
    ✓ Parades / Demonstrations

3 **Disasters (major emergencies generating several incidents)**
    ✓ Earthquake
    ✓ Flood
    ✓ Severe Winter Storms

4 **Routine Incidents (it is of great benefit to use ICS for all incidents)**

Command Considerations

☐ Identify (to the extent possible), all hazardous substances or conditions present.

☐ Implement appropriate emergency operations and ensure that proper personal protective equipment is worn based on the hazard(s) present.

☐ Ensure that emergency responders exposed to potential inhalation hazards wear Self Contained Breathing Apparatus (SCBA) or supplied air respirators, until air monitoring reveals no further hazard.

☐ Limit the number of response personnel in potentially hazardous areas to those who are actively performing emergency operations, but ensure operations in hazardous areas are performed using the "Buddy System" in groups of two (2) or more.

☐ Ensure that backup personnel are standing by with equipment ready to provide assistance or rescue. (If possible, have at least one backup person for each person working in a hazardous area.)

☐ Designate a Safety Officer who is knowledgeable in the operations being implemented at the emergency response site. The Safety Officer has specific responsibility to identify and evaluate hazards and to provide direction with respect to the

safety of operations. The Safety Officer has authority to alter, suspend or terminate any unsafe activities.
❑ Implement appropriate decontamination procedures.
❑ Unified Command must be utilized in terrorist events.
❑ Identify specific tasks prior to assigning resources.
❑ Designate a "Situational Awareness Officer" to focus on all new or additional threats not associated with the incident scene (counter tunnel-vision assignment).

Basic Task Assignments for an Incident Command System

FIRE RESPONSIBILITIES

Fire Attack	Water Supply
Search / Rescue Team	Exposure (Alpha, Bravo, Charlie, Delta)
Evacuation	Division or Sector (A, B, C, D — Sides of structure)
Rapid Intervention Team	Division (1, 2, 3, etc... floors of building)
Safety	Overhaul
Ventilation	Recon

MEDICAL RESPONSIBILITIES

Medical Branch Director	Triage
Treatment	Transportation
Communication	Extrication
Medical Staging	Supply
Landing Zone (LZ)	Recon

HAZMAT TEAM RESPONSIBILITIES

Recon	Safety
Hot, Warm, Cold Zones	Entry Team
Back-up Team	Evacuation
Decon	Containment
Technical Assistance	

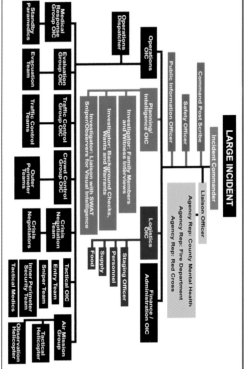

LARGE INCIDENT

- Incident Commander
  - Liaison Officer
    - Agency Rep: County Mental Health
    - Agency Rep: Fire Department
    - Agency Rep: Red Cross
  - Command Post Scribe
  - Safety Officer
  - Public Information Officer
  - Operations OIC
    - Operations Dispatcher
    - Medical Response Group OIC
      - Standby Paramedics
      - Evaluation Group OIC
      - Evacuation Team
    - Traffic Control Group OIC
      - Traffic Control Teams
    - Crowd Control Group OIC
      - Outer Perimeter Teams
  - Planning / Intelligence OIC
    - Investigator: Family Members and Witness Interviews
    - Investigator: Background Checks, Wants and Warrants
    - Investigator: Liaison with SWAT Sniper/Observers for Visual Intelligence
  - Logistics OIC
    - Staging Officer
    - Personnel
    - Supply
    - Food
    - Crisis Negotiation Team
      - Crisis Negotiators
    - Tactical OIC
      - Entry Team
      - Sniper Team
      - Inner Perimeter Security Team
      - Tactical Medics
    - Air Mission Group
      - Tactical Helicopter
      - Observation Helicopter
  - Finance / Administration OIC

34

Unified Operations Section

- The Incident Commander will determine the need for a separate Operation Section at an incident or event. When the Incident Commander activates the Operations Section, he or she will assign an individual to be the Operations Section Chief. If no Operations Section is established, the Incident Commander will maintain direct control of tactical resources.

- The **Operations Section Chief** will develop and manage the Operations Section to accomplish the incident objectives set by the Incident Commander. The Operations Section Chief is normally the person with the greatest technical and tactical expertise in dealing with the problem at hand.

- The **Operations Section Chief** is responsible for developing and implementing strategies and tactics to carry out the incident objectives. The Operations Section Chief's responsibilities include organizing, assigning and supervising all of the tactical field resources assigned to an incident, including air operations and resources in staging areas.

- The **Operations Section Chief** works very closely with other members of the Command and General Staff to coordinate activities.

- The **Operations function** is where tactical fieldwork is done. Therefore, most incident resources are assigned to the Operations Section. Often, the most hazardous activities are carried out there. Because of this, it is necessary to monitor carefully the number of resources that report to any one supervisor.

Planning Section

The **Incident Commander** will determine if there is a need for a Planning Section and designate a Planning Section Chief. If no Planning Section is established, the Incident Commander will perform all planning functions.

It is up to the **Planning Section Chief** to activate any needed additional staffing. Responsibilities of the Planning Section Chief include:

- ✓ Gathering and analyzing information
- ✓ Gathering, analyzing and disseminating intelligence and information
- ✓ Managing the planning process
- ✓ Compiling the Incident Action Plan
- ✓ Developing a written Incident Action Plan (usually done for large incidents and when the Incident Commander has directed)
- ✓ Managing the activities of Technical Specialists
- ✓ Working closely with the Incident Commander and other members of the General Staff to be sure that information is shared effectively and results in an efficient planning process to meet the needs of the Incident Commander and Operations

The major activities of the Planning Section may include:

- ✓ Collecting, evaluating and displaying incident intelligence and information
- ✓ Preparing and documenting Incident Action Plans
- ✓ Conducting long-range and / or contingency planning
- ✓ Developing plans for demobilization as the incident winds down
- ✓ Maintaining incident documentation
- ✓ Tracking resources assigned to the incident

If needed, establish the following:

- ✓ Situation Status (SITSTAT) Unit

✓ Resources Status (RESTAT) Unit
✓ Documentation Unit
✓ Demobilization Unit
✓ Technical Unit

Liaison Officer

The Liaison Officer will determine if there is a need for a Liaison Officer and will designate the Liaison Officer, if so needed. The **Liaison Officer** serves as the primary contact for supporting agencies assisting at an incident.

The Liaison Officer:

✓ Assists the Incident Commander by gathering information about agencies that are supporting our efforts on this incident
✓ Serves as a coordinator for agencies at all levels of
✓ government that are not represented in the command
✓ structure
✓ Provides briefings to agency representatives and works with them to address their questions and concerns about the operation
✓ Confers with agency representatives about restrictions on their resources that may impact how they can be used or special support requirements that they might have
✓ Determines availability of any other specialized resources other agencies might have that may prove useful

Logistics Section

The **Logistics Section Chief** assists the Incident Commander by providing the resources and services required to support incident activities. He or she will coordinate activities very closely with the other members of the Command and General Staff.

the written Incident Action Plan and forwards them to the Planning Section. Logistics and Finance have to work closely to contract for and purchase goods and services needed at the incident.

The Logistics Section is responsible for all of the services and support needs, including:

- ✓ Obtaining, maintaining and accounting for essential personnel, equipment and supplies
- ✓ Providing communication planning and resources
- ✓ Setting up food services
- ✓ Setting up and maintaining incident facilities
- ✓ Providing support transportation
- ✓ Providing medical services to incident personnel

Armorer

1 Responsible for repair and/or replacement of appropriate authorized weapons
2 Reports to the supply unit OIC
3 Determine:
   - ✓ Location of work station
   - ✓ Types and numbers of weapons deployed to the incident
4 Set-up storage / work area
5 Establish inventory and accountability system
6 Obtain spare parts and/or replacement weapons as necessary
7 Receive, replace, or repair all weapons as required
8 Ensure that all appropriate safety measures are taken in work / testing area

Public Information Officer (PIO)

For more information on what types of information should and should not be released, refer to page 66

1 Upon arrival, the **PIO** should contact the Incident Commander (IC) at Command Post to receive briefing:
   ✓ Size and scope of incident
   ✓ Expectations of the IC and PIO
   ✓ Incident objectives
   ✓ Agencies / organizations involved or with vested interest
   ✓ Political subdivisions
   ✓ Current incident activities and situation
   ✓ Special concerns or safety issues

2 Begin preparing PIO worksheet (see page 42).

3 Establish dedicated phone lines for inquiries from the media.

4 Gather basic facts about the incident:
   ✓ Who, What, When and Where
   ✓ Use this information to answer media inquiries

5 With each media contact, record:
   ✓ Name, number and affiliation of caller

6 If a question is asked that you cannot answer, write down and read back - let them know it will be answered later.

7 Select location for Joint Information Center (JIC):
   ✓ Enough space for 12 people to work
   ✓ Minimum of eight (8) AC outlets or power strips.
   ✓ Access to copy machine
   ✓ Location close to but not impinging on Command Post

8 Request necessary support staff through Logistics

1. Assemble the facts into two (2) or three (3) sentences that answer:
   - ✓ Who, What, When and Where
2. List the remaining facts and information in bullet form:
   - ✓ What agencies are responding
   - ✓ Type and amount of equipment
3. Press release should fit on one (1) page.
4. Spell check, edit and give to IC for approval.
5. Provide copy to on scene reporters and fax to all media.
6. Assess public perception of message and report to IC.

PIO Presentations

1. Put yourself in the shoes of the audience and address issues that most concern them.
2. Prepare a statement of commitment, empathy or concern to use as an introduction.

EXAMPLE: "As you are all aware, we are faced with an event that is challenging to our public safety personnel. All parties involved are committed to working in a unified manner to resolve this situation in the most expedient and safest manner possible."

3. Prepare two (2) or three (3) key messages you want to address and incorporate them into a link between your opening statement and the main message.

EXAMPLE: "Our police officers have isolated the problem to the third floor."

4 Repeat your first key message and state two (2) to four (4) facts to support it.

EXAMPLE: "We have established a perimeter around the building. Our tactical officers are in position to resolve the situation peacefully if possible."

5 Repeat Step 4 for other key messages you have prepared.

6 Write a link between the main body of your statement and your conclusion:
   ✓ Repeat your key messages again in the same or similar fashion as Step 3.

7 State future actions as a conclusion.

NOTE: The public will remember what you looked like and how well you spoke. The content of your statement has little impact on public perception. Physical presence is 60%, voice and how you speak is 30%, words and what you say is only 10%. A calm professional manner is contagious - just like panic.

Notes

PIO Worksheet

All written responses for Steps 1 - 7 from the previous pages should be put on this sheet.

STATEMENT

KEY MESSAGE(S)

KEY MESSAGE(S) WITH SUPPORTING FACTS

REPEAT KEY MESSAGE(S)

FUTURE ACTIONS

Routine Incident Guidelines

The following guides are designed to provide guidance for high-risk, fairly low-frequency incidents. These guidelines are not inclusive.

Always adhere to local guidelines and department policies and refer to the **Major Incident Management & Guidelines on page 30.**

General Incident Guidelines

ENSURE OFFICER SAFETY

1 **Evaluate the Scene**
   - ✓ Establish perimeter
   - ✓ Secure, protect and preserve the scene
   - ✓ Protection of citizens and property
2 **Administer First Aid**
   - ✓ Contact EMS
   - ✓ Consider EMS for extended operations
3 **Contact Officer at Scene for Briefing**
   - ✓ Determine type & extent of incident
4 **Select & Set Up Command Post**
   - ✓ Neutral ground, outside perimeter
   - ✓ Staging or assembly area
5 **Identify & Isolate Responsible Parties**
   - ✓ Radio suspect description
6 **Environmental Conditions**
   - ✓ Identify hazards
   - ✓ Evacuation if necessary
7 **Communication of Information**
   - ✓ Develop a plan of action
   - ✓ Establish & communicate objectives to all
8 **Coordinate Operation**
   - ✓ Prepare roster of participating agencies
   - ✓ Establish manpower & equipment needs
9 **Media Relations**
   - ✓ Refer to Press Releases (see page 66) and PIO Presentations (see page 40)

CIVILIAN PLANE: Report time, location, persons injured / killed, and ID# of Aircraft.
MILITARY PLANE: Report time, location, persons injured / killed, home station, and aircraft number. Notify nearest military installation if military not available at scene. Provide guard until relieved. Information released by military only.

ENSURE OFFICER SAFETY

1 Evaluate the Scene
- ✓ Establish perimeter
- ✓ Secure, protect, and preserve the scene
- ✓ Protection of citizens and property
- ✓ Determine if military or civilian aircraft
- ✓ Obtain aircraft information
- ✓ Local military telephone #:

  _____

2 Select & Set Up Command Post
- ✓ Neutral ground, outside perimeter
- ✓ Staging or assembly area

3 Identification of Hazards
- ✓ Geographic location
- ✓ Population area / mountainous / water
- ✓ Environmental conditions / accessibility
- ✓ Cargo (manifest carried)
- ✓ Carbon fiber fumes from prop damage - HAZARD

4 Communication of Information
- ✓ Develop a plan of action
- ✓ Establish & communicate objectives to all

5 Establish Manpower & Equipment Needs

6 Rescue Equipment
- ✓ EMS / Fire Department
- ✓ Search & Rescue team / helicopter

7 Communication Needs
- ✓ Pack sets / portable repeater
- ✓ Satellite phones / cell phones

8 Military Accident
- ✓ Post guard until relieved by military personnel
- ✓ Pilot(s) may be in explosive type ejectable seat

9 Document Manpower & Equipment Use

Child / Elder / Sexual Abuse Investigation

ENSURE OFFICER SAFETY, DO NOT CONFRONT ALLEGED ABUSER OR LEAVE VICTIM ALONE

1 When You Receive the Referral
- ✓ Know department guidelines & State statutes
- ✓ Know what resources are available in your community & provide this information to the victim or child's family if a young minor
- ✓ Introduce yourself, your role, and the focus & objective of investigation
- ✓ Assure the best treatment for protection of the victim
- ✓ Interview victim alone, focusing on corroborative evidence

2 Information for the Preliminary Report
- ✓ Inquire about the history of the abusive situation
  - Times/dates are important to set the timeline
- ✓ Cover the elements of crime necessary for report
  - Inquire about the instrument of abuse
  - Inquire about other items of the scene
- ✓ Don't discount victim's statements about:
  - Who is abusing them
  - How the abuse is occurring
  - What types of acts occurred
- ✓ Save opinions for end of the report
  - Provide supportive facts

3 Preserving the Crime Scene
  ✓ Treat the scene as a crime scene
    • Not as the site of a social problem
    • Even if abuse has occurred in the past

NOTE: If sexual abuse is suspected, do not allow the victim to wash. Contact the proper services to immediately perform a medical sexual assault evaluation.

  ✓ Secure
    • Instrument of abuse
    • Other corroborative evidence from the victim
  ✓ Photograph scene & injuries to victim
    • Rephotograph injuries to capture changes
4 Follow-up Investigation
  ✓ Be supportive & optimistic to victim & family
  ✓ Arrange for medical exam & transportation
    • Collect clothing for evidence if necessary
  ✓ Link victim & family to support services in your area

Civil Disturbance

ENSURE OFFICER SAFETY

1 Containment of Incident
  ✓ Check for injuries
  ✓ Check for property damage
  ✓ Check for occurring criminal activity
2 Select & Set Up Command Post
  ✓ Neutral ground, outside perimeter
  ✓ Staging or assembly area
  ✓ Keep safe routes to and from scene open
  ✓ Video or photographic record of incident
3 Identification of Hazards
  ✓ Chemical
  ✓ Population area / mountainous / water

 ✓ Environmental conditions / accessibility
 ✓ Fire
 ✓ Explosives
4 **Establish Manpower & Equipment Needs**
 ✓ Fire Department / EMS
 ✓ Aircraft
 ✓ Riot Squad
 ✓ Telephones
 ✓ Pack sets / portable repeater
 ✓ Satellite phones / cell phones
5 **Identify & Contact Property Owner**
6 **Identify & Contact Protest Leader(s) and / or Suspects**
 ✓ Photograph protest leader(s) and / or suspects
 ✓ Determine cause of protest
 ✓ Announcement of dispersal unlawful or riotous assemblages
7 **Protect Department Property From Damage**
8 **Media Control**

Courtroom Testimony—Speeding

Speed offense cases have four (4) elements — It is essential to establish every element to convict!

1 **Device Confirmation**
 ✓ Steady readout from unit
 ✓ Readout consistent with visual estimation
2 **Driver** Establish that accused was operating vehicle
3 **Vehicle**
 ✓ Establish that vehicle was used to commit the violation
 ✓ Establish that speed measurement(s) came from that vehicle
4 **Location**
 ✓ Establish location of violation & venue

- Absolute limit
- Prima facia limit

5 Speed Measuring Devices
- ✓ Supply evidence in support of the speed element
- ✓ To be admissible radar speed measurement must have been obtained in compliance with case law:
  - Radar was operating properly
  - Device's accuracy was verified using an appropriate and acceptable method
  - The operator was properly qualified and trained
  - Violation was observed by operator
  - Operator made a visual estimate of the target vehicle's speed

Case Law

1 *State v. Dantonio* (New Jersey)
- ✓ First judicial notice taken of Doppler Principal

2 *State v. Tomanelli* (Connecticut)
- ✓ 152 365, 216, A2d 625
- ✓ Tuning fork method as a reliable test of accuracy

3 *Royals v. Commonwealth* (Virginia)
- ✓ Established that test of accuracy of a radar device should be done each time the device was set up for use at a particular location during a duty shift.

4 *Thomas v. City of Norfolk* (Virginia)
- ✓ Relaxed stationary radar testing criteria
- ✓ Test at beginning and end of duty shift

5 *Honeycutt v. Commonwealth* (Kentucky)
- ✓ 408 SW2d 421 (November 4, 1966)
- ✓ Operator must:
  - Set up radar device properly

- Test device properly to verify it is working
- Read device properly to obtain measurement

✓ Verification that measurement came from target:
  - Vehicle must be closest to the radar
  - Must be out in front of and separated from other vehicles
  - Operator should have visual estimate of speed
  - Radar measurement should be close to estimate

6 *State v. Hanson* (Wisconsin)
  ✓ Establishes moving radar operational requirements

Courtroom Testimony—General

1 Preparing For Court
  ✓ Review report, evidence, scene, law
  ✓ Review departmental procedures
  ✓ Review spelling / pronunciation of technical terms
  ✓ Pre-trial conference with prosecutor
  ✓ Be on time for court

2 Prepare Current Résumé or Curriculum Vitae (CV)
  ✓ Ensures consistency of testimony
  ✓ Documents education, training, experience, prior testimony, awards, writings, presentations, etc.
  ✓ Essential for professional credibility

3 Appearance
  ✓ First impressions are lasting impressions
  ✓ Prepare as you would for promotional interview
  ✓ If plain clothes — dress conservatively
  ✓ Well groomed

4 Avoid
  ✓ Fancy jewelry, big belt buckles, cowboy boots, sun glasses, logo-wear
  ✓ Jangling keys & coins, handcuff tie-clasps, "pig" tie-clasps, non-issue lapel pins

5 Writing For Court

- ✓ Avoid congregating
- ✓ Avoid jokes & laughing
- ✓ Your credibility is being assessed

6 Entry Into The Courtroom
- ✓ Jurors first opportunity to assess you
- ✓ Stand straight / shoulders back
- ✓ OK to glance at the jury
- ✓ Avoid nods, smirks, smiles, the "look" to the defendant

7 Be A Good Witness, be:
- ✓ Calm, self-controlled, self-assured, & knowledgeable
- ✓ Prepared, not arrogant, not a know-it-all, be human
- ✓ Humble, respect the system & its participants

8 Testifying
- ✓ Culmination of case — allows you to teach

Crime Scene Guidelines

ENSURE OFFICER SAFETY

1 Follow Universal Precautions (see page 80)

2 Secure Scene
- ✓ Control access to scene
- ✓ Maintain scene access log

3 Select & Set Up Command Post
- ✓ Neutral ground, outside perimeter
- ✓ Staging or assembly area
- ✓ Keep safe routes to and from scene open
- ✓ Video or photographic record of incident

4 Team Leader
- ✓ Oversee entire crime scene operation
- ✓ Determine team assignments
- ✓ Assign search patterns

5 Establish Manpower & Equipment Needs
- ✓ Fire Department / EMS

- ✓ Crime Scene Unit
- ✓ Telephones
- ✓ Pack sets / Portable repeater
- ✓ Satellite phones, Cell phones

6 Photographer
- ✓ Photograph all evidence before collection

7 Scene Diagrammer
- ✓ Make diagram of scene include major objects
- ✓ Take measurements - double check each one

8 Evidence Custodian / Recorder
- ✓ Document on evidence container:
  - Date & time
  - Location of collection
  - Initials
- ✓ Package evidence to maintain integrity
- ✓ Maintain evidence log

9 Media Control

Crime Scene Investigation

ENSURE OFFICER SAFETY

1 Initial Response
- ✓ Note dispatch information
- ✓ Be aware of persons and vehicles leaving the scene
- ✓ Approach with caution
- ✓ Scan area thoroughly - note secondary crime scenes
- ✓ Be aware of persons / vehicles that may be involved
- ✓ Make initial observations (look, listen, smell) to assess the scene and ensure officer safety
- ✓ Remain alert & attentive
- ✓ Assume the crime is ongoing until determined otherwise
- ✓ Treat as crime scene until otherwise determined

2 Safety Procedures

DNA Evidence

1 **Avoid Contamination**
   - ✓ Wear gloves — change them often
   - ✓ Use disposable instruments or clean them thoroughly before & after handling each sample
   - ✓ Avoid touching area where you believe DNA may exist
   - ✓ Avoid talking, sneezing, & coughing over evidence
   - ✓ Avoid touching your face, nose, and mouth when collecting & packaging evidence
   - ✓ Air-dry evidence thoroughly before packaging
   - ✓ Put evidence into new paper bags or envelopes
   - ✓ DO NOT use plastic bags
   - ✓ DO NOT use staples

2 **Transportation & Storage**
   - ✓ Keep evidence dry & at room temperature
   - ✓ Once packaged - seal & label

3 **Document**
   - ✓ Location found
   - ✓ Chain of custody

4 **Collect Elimination Sample(s)**
   - ✓ Determines if DNA is from suspect or other(s)
   - ✓ Used for comparison
   - ✓ Homicide: victim (even if decomposed)
   - ✓ Rape: victim's recent consensual partners (approach victim with extreme sensitivity & provide full explanation for request. Consider having victim advocate present)
   - ✓ Burglary: other persons at residence / building

ICS

5 DNA in the Human Body
   ✓ Blood / semen / saliva
   ✓ Skin Cells / tissue / organ / muscle
   ✓ Brain cells / bone / teeth / hair
   ✓ Mucus / perspiration
   ✓ Fingernails
   ✓ Urine / feces / etc.

Sample Size of DNA

Only a few cells are needed to obtain a userful sample. On the next page is a list of some common items of evidence that you may need to collect, the possible location of the DNA, and the biological source. Just because you cannot see a stain does not mean that there are not enough cells for DNA typing.

Notes

Identifying DNA Evidence

Evidence	Location of DNA	Source of DNA
Baseball bat, similar weapon	Handle, end	Sweat, skin, blood, tissue
Hat, bandana, mask	Inside	Sweat, hair, dandruff
Eyeglasses	Nose or ear pieces, lenses	Sweat, skin
Facial tissue, cotton swabs	Surface area	Mucus, blood, sweat, semen, ear wax
Dirty laundry	Surface area	Blood, sweat, semen
Toothpick	Tips	Saliva
Smoked cigarette	Cigarette butt	Saliva
Stamp or envelope	Licked area	Saliva
Tape or ligature	Inside/outside surface	Skin, sweat
Bottle, can, or drinking glass	Sides, rim, opening	Saliva, sweat
Used condom	Inside/outside surface	Semen, vaginal, or rectal cells
Blanket, pillow, sheet	Surface area	Sweat, hair, semen, urine, saliva
"Through and through" bullet	Outside surface	Blood, tissue
Bite mark	Person's skin or clothing	Saliva

56

Domestic Violence

ENSURE OFFICER SAFETY

1 Separate and Interview Both Parties
   - ✓ Determine need for medical attention / EMS
   - ✓ Tape record interview(s)
   - ✓ Describe and photograph victim, suspect, & scene
   - ✓ Interview other witnesses including children
   - ✓ Determine primary aggressor
2 Determine Addition Charges
   - ✓ Weapons
   - ✓ Drugs
   - ✓ Neglect
3 Provide Information On
   - ✓ Victim's rights
   - ✓ Restraining orders
   - ✓ Other available devices / services
4 Consider Preventative Actions
   - ✓ Transport
   - ✓ Call a friend, etc.
5 Note on Report Availability of
   - ✓ 9-1-1 tapes
   - ✓ Medical records
6 Does Victim Request Notification if Suspect is Released From custody?
7 Identify Yourself and Agency
   - ✓ Provide phone number where you can be contacted
   - ✓ Provide agency case number

Crisis Center:

Domestic Violence Shelter:

Victim's Assistance:

Lab, biological weapons, radiological or
chemical threat, contact proper agency prior to entry
- ✓ Approach in a manner to reduce risk to officer(s)
- ✓ Maximize safety of victims, witnesses, and others
- ✓ Survey for dangerous persons & control situation
- ✓ Notify Supervisor
- ✓ Call for assistance / backup

3 Emergency Care
- ✓ Assess victim(s) for signs of life & medical needs
- ✓ Notify EMS
- ✓ Guide EMS to victim to minimize contamination
- ✓ Point out potential physical evidence to EMS - instruct them to minimize contact with evidence
- ✓ Document removal of persons / items by EMS
- ✓ DO NOT let EMS "clean-up" the scene
- ✓ Document EMS personnel - name, unit, phone, etc.
- ✓ Attempt to obtain "dying declaration" if appropriate
- ✓ Document statements / comments by victims, suspects, or witnesses at the scene
- ✓ If victim / suspect is transported by EMS, send officer with EMS to document comments made and preserve evidence. If no officer available, stay at scene and instruct EMS to preserve evidence

4 Secure & Control Persons at Scene
- ✓ Control all individuals at the scene
- ✓ Prevent from altering / destroying evidence
- ✓ Identify all individuals at the scene, such as:
  - **Suspects:** secure & separate
  - **Witnesses:** secure & separate
  - **Bystanders:** remove if not a witness
  - **Victims / Family / Friends:** control w/compassion
  - **Medial and other assisting personnel**

✓ Exclude unauthorized and nonessential personnel from the scene (e.g., law enforcement officials not working the case, politicians, media)

Controlling the movement of persons at the crime scene and limiting the number of persons who enter the crime scene is essential to maintaining scene integrity, safeguarding evidence, and minimizing contamination.

5 **Identify, Establish, Protect, & Secure Scene Boundaries**

6 **Turn Over Control of the Scene and Brief Investigator(s)**

7 **Document Actions and Observations**

8 **Preliminary Documentation & Evaluation of the Scene**
   ✓ Conduct scene assessment
   ✓ Conduct "walk-through" and initial documentation

9 **Processing the Scene**
   ✓ Determine team composition
   ✓ Contamination control
   ✓ Documentation
   ✓ Prioritize collection of evidence
   ✓ Collect, preserve, inventory, package, transport, and submit evidence

10 **Completing and Recording Crime Scene Investigation**
   ✓ Establish crime scene debriefing team
   ✓ Perform final survey of the crime scene
   ✓ Complete documentation of the crime scene.

040-049	Connecticut	530	Nevada
050-134	New York	531-539	Washington
135-158	New Jersey	540-544	Oregon
159-211	Pennsylvania	545-573	California
212-220	Maryland	574	Alaska
221-222	Delaware	575-576	Hawaii
223-231	Virginia	577-579	Washington DC
232-236	West Virginia	580[1]	Virgin Islands
232	North Carolina	580-584	Puerto Rico
237-246	North Carolina	585	New Mexico
247-251	South Carolina	586[1]	Guam, American Samoa Northern Mariana Islands, Philippines
252-260	Georgia	587-588	Mississippi
261-267	Florida	589-595	Florida
268-302	Ohio	596-599	Puerto Rico
302-317	Indiana	600-601	Arizona
318-361	Illinois	602-626	California
362-386	Michigan	627-645	Texas
387-399	Wisconsin	646-647	Utah
400-407	Kentucky	648-649	New Mexico
408-415	Tennessee	650-653	Colorado
416-424	Alabama	654-658	South Carolina
425-428	Mississippi	659-658	Colorado
429-432	Arkansas	667-675	Georgia

433-439	Louisiana	676-679	Arkansas
440-448	Oklahoma	680	Nevada

449-467	Texas	691-699	Not Assigned
468-477	Minnesota	700-728	Railroad Board
478-485	Iowa	750-751	Hawaii

486-500	Missouri	752-755	Mississippi
501-502	North Dakota	756-763	Tennessee
503-504	South Dakota	764-765	Arizona
505-508	Nebraska	766-772	Florida
509-515	Kansas	[1]Some numbers from this area also assigned to SE Asian refugees from 75-79	
516-517	Montana		
518-519	Idaho	[2]Not issued in the US since 1960'2	

Notes